Joe Franklin's
Movie Trivia

ALSO BY JOE FRANKLIN

Joe Franklin's Encyclopedia of Comedians
A Gift for People
The Memory Lane Cookbook

Joe Franklin's

Movie Trivia

HASTINGS HOUSE
Book Publishers
Mamaroneck, NY

Library of Congress Catalog Card Number 92-081635
ISBN 0-8038-9348-3

Caricatures by Gerry Hoylie

Photos courtesy of the Joe Franklin movie archives

This book is dedicated to my mentors,
Eddie Cantor and Martin Block.

ACKNOWLEDGMENTS

This is to acknowledge the work of Gigi Foger who toiled many a night to bring this project together. I would also like to thank Vallerie Lynn Huyghue of Hastings House for her sharp editorial eye and sense of humor while blue penciling the manuscript.

DISCLAIMER

Any stars whose names I've misspelled, should change the spelling of their names.

Any star whom I misplaced by a decade, well, I owe you ten years.

Any star who feels left out, not to worry, I intend to use you in my next book—The Son of Movie Trivia.

Contents

Are Film Stars Real People?

In my forty years as a talk-show host on radio and TV, I've chatted with more stars than there are in heaven. I get to see their human side, be they laughing or crying—like Bing Crosby, singing on my show all night, without an orchestra, forgetting lines and faking it and having a helluva time.

When Bill Cosby was a nightclub comedian, I was the first one to put him on the air. He's been on my show hundreds of times. He loves coming back to sit with me during the late hours of the show so we can talk. I told him, "I'm going to bequeath my show to you when I retire."

Myrna Loy has been on the show frequently. People forget that she was once named the Queen of Hollywood. They don't know that after the bombing of Pearl Harbor she took a leave of absence from movies to volunteer for the Red Cross. After her movie career she devoted her life to work for the United Nations.

The public often forgets that actors and actresses in movies are real people, even though fans glamorize the stars into the personas of their movie roles. Roger Moore may have played the role of James Bond on the screen, but off the screen he'd rather crack jokes and be a comedian. He never loses an opportunity to be on the dais at a Friar's roast, lampooning the hell out of a fellow performer.

Boris Karloff, the late master of menace who created horror movies with his performance in *Frankenstein*, was involved in many acts of charity for underprivileged children and raised orchids as a hobby. Jerry Lewis has starred in and directed movies and teaches film at universities. Now he devotes himself to voluntary fund-raising for the Muscular Dystrophy Association as a full-time endeavor.

Few people know that Humphrey Bogart, when in the U.S. Navy in World War I, was wounded while serving on the *Leviathan*. It scarred his upper lip, which accounted for his slight lisp. In a way, Bogart owes some of his success to the integrity and friendship of fellow actor Leslie Howard. They played opposite each other in the Broadway success

The Petrified Forest. When Warners bought the rights for the movie to star Leslie Howard, it offered the Bogart role to Edward G. Robinson. Howard stood up to the studio and said, "I refuse to play in the film unless Bogart gets the part." The studio gave in, the film was successful, and Bogart went on to stardom.

During the 1960 presidential election, after one of the famous political debates between Nixon and Kennedy, the two men walked by the studio where I was broadcasting. I waved them in to say hello, and like the two friends they really were, they sat down, and we had the damnedest talk show of all time. Not one word of politics, just family stuff and humorous anecdotes and joking like a couple of comedians.

Bob Hope never fails to stop in when he's in New York. He doesn't do it for the money—we don't pay anything— he's just a long-time friend who likes our homey atmosphere. Billy Crystal is another comedian/actor who never fails to stop by to chat. Of course, I knew him ever since his father owned the music store where I got my records.

As for Madonna, her first broadcast was on my show. Not only that, when I needed help in the office, she'd roll up her sleeves, type letters, and answer the phone. I don't have to ask why because she summed it up recently when she said, "His office looks like a flea market and his show is like being home—like wearing a pair of old comfortable shoes."

Even the one and only Charlie Chaplin used to come in to talk to me and let his hair down. He liked to do English vaudeville shtick. Brooklyn boy Jimmy Cagney loved to shmooze about old New York, while John Wayne, an Iowa boy, talked about his getting a football scholarship to USC—when his name was still Marion Michael Morrison. Shirley Temple Black, even after she was our United Nations ambassador, would drop by and chat about the good old days.

I'm what is known as a comfortable guy, so it's natural for me to be comfortable with the stars and vice versa. The first show Elvis Presley appeared on was mine. He was heard by a network executive and booked on Steve Allen's "Tonight Show" followed by "The Ed Sullivan Show." The rest is history, but even then, Elvis returned to my show from time to time—even when he was a corporal in the army—as his way of saying thanks.

My fondest memories probably are of the late Jayne Mansfield. Everyone used to think she was a dumb blonde with big boobs. Few people knew she had a genius I.Q. of 168, so she outsmarted Hollywood and did unto Hollywood what Hollywood had been doing to the public for years—she hyped her own career.

Oscar Levant once said about Hollywood, "Underneath that phony tinsel of Hollywood you'll find the real tinsel."

My experiences are different. Underneath the tinsel you find the real people who, even when they're hurting, put on makeup and make us laugh, cry, and, on occasion, think. They love to be on stage every minute—and hope you love them when they are.

—Joe Franklin

Questions

The 1920s

1

In what movie does Al Jolson say: "You ain't seen nothing yet"?

2

What actor starred in The Mark of Zorro?

3

Clara Bow, Antonio Moreno, William Austin, Jane Daily, and Gary Cooper starred in what 1927 movie?

4

Who was Greta Garbo's lover in the film A Woman of Affairs?

5

What male actor's popularity peaked after playing opposite Greta Garbo in such films as The Merry Widow, Le Bohème, and Queen Christina?

6

Name Joan Crawford's first talkie.

Greta Garbo

7

Two pilots vie for the attention of the "It" girl in the movie *Wings*. Can you name them?

8

Who won the first Oscar for Best Actress, in 1927–1928?

a) Louise Dressler
b) Janet Gaynor
c) Gloria Swanson
d) Joan Crawford

9

Charlton Heston played the title role in the 1959 epic *Ben Hur*. Who played the role in the 1926 silent version of the same movie?

10

Identify the actress who starred in the following films: *Mantrap*, *Wings*, and *The Wild Party*.

a) Gloria Swanson
b) Clara Bow
c) Bette Davis
d) Joan Crawford

11

Who played Quasimodo in the original silent-movie version of *The Hunchback of Notre Dame*?

12

Name the only silent movie to win an Academy Award in 1928.

13

Born Gladys Smith, she went on to become a famous star. What was her stage name?

14

Al Jolson first sang "Sonny Boy" in what film?

15

Name the first musical to win a Best Picture Academy Award.

16

What silent film classic features Laura LaPlante and a group of nervous people who are forced to spend a night in a haunted house?

17

Identify the silent Hitchcock film in which Betty Balfour's father pretends he's broke in order to teach her a lesson.

18

Name the Marx Brothers' first movie.

19

In what movie does Buster Keaton become an all-star athlete in order to please his girlfriend, played by Ann Cornwall?

20

Which actress starred in *Dancing Mothers?*

    a) Joan Crawford
    b) Clara Bow
    c) Lillian Gish
    d) Margaret Lindsay
    e) Virginia Bruce

21

Name the silent comedy about the army that starred Wallace Beery, Mary Brian, and Raymond Hatton.

22

Who starred in *The Beloved Rogue*, the story of poet-adventurer François Villon involved in a battle of wits with Louis XI?

23

Who played the hero and the heroine in *The Big Parade*, a movie featuring some of the most realistic battle scenes ever filmed?

24

Identify the Hitchcock film in which a young woman kills the man who tries to rape her and becomes trapped between a police investigation and a blackmailer.

25

Who played the male lead as a bullfighter in *Blood and Sand*?

   a) Errol Flynn
   b) Edward G. Robinson
   c) John Longden
   d) Donald Caithrop
   e) Rudolph Valentino

The 1930s

1

In what film was a conscientious police officer, played by Edmond O'Brien, responsible for Humphrey Bogart's imprisonment?

2

What three actresses portrayed show-girl roommates in *Gold Diggers*?

3

The Academy Award, or the Oscar, is a metal statuette plated with gold. However, there was one occasion when a wooden statue was awarded. Can you name the recipient of the Oscar and why it was wood?

4

In what movie does Joan Crawford dance with Fred Astaire? (The movie also starred Clark Gable, Franchot Tone, and Nelson Eddy.)

5

For which movie did Clark Gable win his only Academy Award for Best Actor?

a) *Gone With the Wind*
b) *The Misfits*
c) *It Happened One Night*
d) *Saratoga*

Clark Gable

13

6

In what movie does Groucho Marx say to Margaret Dumont: "It's the old, old story; boy meets girl, Romeo and Juliet, Minneapolis and St. Paul"?

7

Who played the role of Heathcliff in *Wuthering Heights*?

8

Name the two actors who captured King Kong and brought him to civilization.

9

Name the movie with Eleanor Powell, James Stewart, and Virginia Bruce that featured the songs "I've Got You Under My Skin" and "It's De-Lovely."

10

Who won the Best Actor Oscar in 1932 for portraying a monster and what was the film?

11

Wallace Beery won Best Actor in 1931 for what film?

12

Name the movie in which Marie Dressler says to Madge Evans: "If there's one thing I know it's men. I ought to know. It's been my life's work."

13

In what film did Sabu make his screen debut?

14

Identify the actresses who won Oscars for their performances in *Jezebel*.

15

Name Sonja Henie's first movie. It starred Don Ameche and The Ritz Brothers.

16

Name the actress who portrayed Cary Grant's wife in *Topper*.

17

For what 1938 film did Alice Brady win the Best Supporting Actress Oscar?

15

18

"I always look good when I'm near death," said Greta Garbo. In what movie?

19

In what film did Jeanette MacDonald and Nelson Eddy sing "Indian Love Call"?

20

In the movie King Kong, what was the name of the character played by Fay Wray?

21

Laurel and Hardy's most acclaimed film featured the duo as a couple of conventioneers. Name the film.

22

Busby Berkeley's first film assignment was staging the musical numbers for what Eddie Cantor movie?

23

What sultry actress sang "See What the Boys in the Back Room Will Have" in the film Destry Rides Again?

24

Name the producer of the classic motion picture *Gone With the Wind*.

25

In the film version of her stage play *Diamond Lil*, Mae West invites Cary Grant to her boudoir with: "Come up and see me sometime." Name the movie.

Mae West

26

Who starred in the movies *Thin Ice* and *My Lucky Star*?

27

Who was Clark Gable's female co-star in the movie *Too Hot to Handle*?

28

Which movie won the 1937 Academy Award for Best Picture?

  a) *Captains Courageous*
  b) *The Awful Truth*
  c) *Dead End*
  d) *The Good Earth*
  e) *The Life of Emile Zola*
  f) *In Old Chicago*

29

Who won the Best Actress Oscar for *It Happened One Night*?

30

In what film does Marlene Dietrich portray a street walker who in the end is shot for treason?

31

"Me Tarzan . . . you Jane" was the famous line from the 1932 movie *Tarzan, the Ape Man*. Who played Tarzan and Jane?

32

In what movie does Mae West say to Charles Osgood: "Is that a gun in your pocket or are you glad to see me"?

33

"How do you live?" "I steal . . ." These were the final lines from what 1932 film that starred Paul Muni, Glenda Farrell, Helen Vinson, and Allen Jenkins?

34

Name the actor and actress who starred in the movie *Artists and Models Abroad*.

35

In what 1935 movie does Shirley Temple sing "When I Grow Up"?

36

Name the first film to win these five Oscars: Best Actor, Best Actress, Best Director, Best Screenplay, and Best Picture.

37

Who played the saloon boss Gus Jordan in the movie *She Done Him Wrong?*

38

In what movie does Marlene Dietrich introduce the song "Falling in Love Again"?

39

Who was the only actor ever to win two consecutive Best Actor Oscars, in 1937 and 1938?

40

Further to Question 39, for what movies did he win the awards?

41

What is the title of the movie in which Charlie Chaplin falls in love with a blind flower girl?

42

In what Busby Berkeley movie was "By a Waterfall" performed?

43

Who starred with Marlene Dietrich in *Desire*?

44

What was Humphrey Bogart's 1930 Fox film debut?

45

The song "I've Got You Under My Skin" was introduced in what MGM musical?

46

Who played the role of Quasimodo in the 1939 film version of *The Hunchback of Notre Dame*?

47

Who played the Wizard in *The Wizard of Oz*?

48

Who starred with Buster Keaton in the 1933 film *What! No Beer?*

49

For what film did Helen Hayes receive her Best Actress Academy Award?

50

Stage Struck was the remake of what Katharine Hepburn film?

51

Who sang "Get Thee Behind Me, Satan" in the 1936 movie *Follow the Fleet*, with Fred Astaire, Ginger Rogers, and Randolph Scott.

52

Name Katharine Hepburn's male co-star in the movie *Mary of Scotland*.

53

In what film does Judy Garland sing "Dear Mr. Gable"?

54

In what movie did Humphrey Bogart appear with Gabriel Dell, Leo Gorcey, Huntz Hall, and Bobby Jordan?

55

How many roles did Frank Morgan play in The Wizard of Oz? Can you name them?

56

What actor's first film had him starring in The Invisible Man?

57

Humphrey Bogart played Sam Spade opposite Sidney Greenstreet, but who played Sam Spade in the 1931 version of the movie The Maltese Falcon?

58

William Powell starred as Nick Charles in what film?

59

Name the actor who was supposed to play Robin Hood in the 1938 movie before Errol Flynn got the part.

60

Name the 1935 movie that starred Irene Dunne, Robert Taylor, Betty Furness, and Charles Butterworth.

61

What is the title of the only film that teamed up Spencer Tracy and Humphrey Bogart?

62

Name the 1939 classic that starred Merle Oberon, Laurence Olivier, David Niven, Flora Robeson, and Geraldine Fitzgerald.

63

Who sang "My Old Flame" with Duke Ellington's Orchestra in the movie *Belle of the Nineties?*

64

What is the title of the movie featuring Cary Grant and Douglas Fairbanks, Jr., that is loosely based on a famous Rudyard Kipling poem?

65

Name the first swashbuckler hit for Errol Flynn.

66

In what 1939 film did Maureen O'Hara make her American debut?

67

Name the film that starred Tyrone Power and Myrna Loy, and earned an Academy Award for special effects (the earthquake scenes).

68

Name the 1939 movie starring Gary Cooper, Ray Milland, and Robert Preston that tells the story of three devoted brothers serving in the Foreign Legion under a martinet commander?

69

Clark Gable, Myrna Loy, Spencer Tracy, and Lionel Barrymore were cast in what film featuring daredevils trying out new aircraft?

70

Who starred as Edmond Dantes in the classic swashbuckler *The Count of Monte Cristo*?

   a) Errol Flynn
   b) Ray Milland
   c) Dirk Bogarde
   d) Robert Donat

71

In what film does Ronald Colman star in which an airplane crash in the Tibetan mountains causes four people to be taken by the natives to a Utopian civilization?

72

Who was the lanky dancer in *The Great Ziegfeld* who also appeared in *The Wizard of Oz*?

73

Which one of the following movies did actor/singer/dancer George Raft not appear in?

   a) *Folies Bergère*
   b) *Love Me Tonight*
   c) *Pennies from Heaven*
   d) *The Merry Widow*
   e) *Playboy of Paris*

74

Name the film that first teamed Ginger Rogers and Fred Astaire (they do the Carioca).

75

What actor starred in *Alexander's Ragtime Band*?

76

In what gangster movie does James Cagney squash a grapefruit in Mae Clarke's face?

a) Each Dawn I Die
b) Public Enemy
c) The Roaring Twenties
d) G-Men
e) Angels with Dirty Faces

Jimmy Cagney

77

In what film does Edward G. Robinson pretend to leave the police force in order to crack a citywide mob ring run by Barton MacLane?

78

Name the Mexican-born actor in The Plainsman and Union Pacific.

79

Who starred in the early Western classic Cimarron?

a) John Wayne
b) Errol Flynn
c) Lee Marvin
d) Richard Dix
e) Clark Gable

80

Who received an Oscar for Best Supporting Actor for his role as Doc Boone in Stagecoach?

81

What distinguished actor portrayed the title role in The Werewolf of London?

82

Dick Powell sang "I Only Have Eyes for You" to Ruby Keeler in what movie?

The 1940s

1

The song "Puttin' on the Ritz" is from what movie starring Bing Crosby, Fred Astaire, and Joan Caulfield?

2

Who starred in the title role as boxer Jim Corbett in the movie *Gentleman Jim*?

3

Barbara Stanwyck plays the wife and Burt Lancaster the husband intent on murder in what 1940s suspense thriller? The film also featured the following: Ann Richards, Wendell Corey, Ed Begley, Leif Ericson, and William Conrad.

4

In 1940, the nominees for Best Actor were:

a) Charlie Chaplin, *The Great Dictator*
b) Henry Fonda, *The Grapes of Wrath*
c) Raymond Massey, *Abe Lincoln in Illinois*
d) Laurence Olivier, *Rebecca*
e) James Stewart, *The Philadelphia Story*

Name the winner.

Barbara Stanwyck and Bob Cummings

5

In what film do Ruth Hussey and Ray Milland play brother and sister trying to help a girl tormented by the spirit of her dead mother?

6

Clark Gable and Lana Turner appeared together for the first time in what romantic Western?

7

Identify the only actor ever to win two Oscars for the same role, in 1947.

8

In *Mighty Joe Young*, who played the song "Beautiful Dreamer" in a nightclub when the gorilla went bananas?

9

Who directed all the Henry Aldrich movies in the 1940s?

10

Humphrey Bogart said, regarding the character played by Edward G. Robinson: "One Rocco more or less isn't worth dying for." Name the movie.

11

In what film did John Garfield receive an Oscar nomination for Best Actor in 1947?

12

In 1942 Gary Cooper won the Oscar for Best Actor. Name the movie.

13

In the movie *Along Came Jones*, Gary Cooper plays a mild-mannered cowboy mistaken for a ruthless gunslinger. Name this vicious killer.

14

What actor sang and played "As Time Goes By" in the movie *Casablanca*?

15

In what movie does Rudy Vallee say to Claudette Colbert: "Chivalry is not dead, it's decomposed"?

16

Who won the Best Actress Oscar for *The Farmer's Daughter*?

17

Name the actress who tries to take Spencer Tracy away from Katharine Hepburn in *State of the Union*.

18

Name the actor whose weird laugh made him a star in his first movie, *Kiss of Death*.

19

In what film did Rita Hayworth sing "Put the Blame on Mame"?

20

Who shot Jennifer Jones to death in the film *Duel in the Sun*?

21

What movie featured the song "Zip-Ah-Dee-Doo-Dah"?

22

What actors play Dracula and the Werewolf in *Abbott and Costello Meet Frankenstein*?

23

Who portrayed Al Jolson's wife in *The Jolson Story*?

24

In what film do Joan Crawford and Fred MacMurray embark on a spy mission during their European honeymoon?

25

In *The Accused*, name the actress who portrays a teacher who accidentally kills a student in love with her?

26

Who stars in *Across the Pacific*?

   a) George Sanders
   b) Fredric March
   c) Robert Cummings
   d) Basil Rathbone
   e) Humphrey Bogart

27

What actor, who later played the role of Dracula, has a brief appearance as a dapper stage-door Johnnie in *The Gay Lady*?

28

What was the title of the 1946 remake of *Super Sleuth*?

29

In *Helene*, what talented young actress plays cupid between her widower father, Herbert Marshall, and Laraine Day?

30

Identify the movie in which Gene Raymond plays a stockbroker who steals his firm's money and goes to Hawaii.

31

What movie, based on a book by John Steinbeck, stars Myrna Loy and Robert Mitchum?

  a) *The Grapes of Wrath*
  b) *The Red Pony*
  c) *Tortilla Flat*
  d) *Cannery Row*
  e) *The Wayward Bus*

32

What 1940 Disney movie merged animation with classical music?

33

Lon Chaney, Jr., plays a blind man accused of murdering his girlfriend's father to obtain his eyes for a transplant. Name the movie.

34

What actress plays the domineering wife who hypnotizes Bela Lugosi into a murder plot in *The Invisible Ghost*?

35

What actor and actress dance to Cole Porter music in *The Pirate*, directed by Vincente Minnelli?

Spencer Tracy

36

Who directed *State of the Union*, with Spencer Tracy, Katharine Hepburn, and Angela Lansbury?

37

Who plays Hume Cronyn's daughter in *The Green Years*?

38

Clark Gable pursues Hedy Lamarr, a Russian streetcar conductor, in what film?

39

Who starred in and directed *The Lady from Shanghai* with Rita Hayworth?

40

In what comedy did Dean Martin and Jerry Lewis make their film debut?

41

What actor starred with Humphrey Bogart in the 1949 movie *Knock on Any Door*?

42

In Otto Preminger's film *Fallen Angel*, who kills Linda Darnell, then sets about solving her murder?

43

Who won the Oscar for Best Actor in the motion picture *A Double Life*?

44

What song, written in the 1930s, became the title of the 1944 movie starring Ginger Rogers, Joseph Cotten, and Shirley Temple?

45

In what movie starring Alice Faye and Don Ameche does Carmen Miranda sing "I, Yi, Yi, Yi"?

46

"How would you like to tussle with Russell" was part of an $800,000 ad campaign for the debut of what Jane Russell movie?

47

Name the actor who sang "How I Won the War" in the movie *Thank Your Lucky Stars*.

48

What 1942 movie starred James Cagney and also featured a small role played by his sister Jeanne Cagney?

49

"You must come up and see me sometime" was a line from the movie *My Little Chickadee*. Who said the line and to whom?

50

The following stellar cast was featured in what 1940s flick: Spencer Tracy, Irene Dunne, Van Johnson, Ward Bond, James Gleason, Lionel Barrymore, and Esther Williams?

51

Identify the 1943 film whose ad coyly asks: "What are the two great reasons for Jane Russell's rise to stardom?" Censors said of the movie: "Jane Russell's breasts hung over the film like a thunderstorm spread out over a landscape."

52

Who plays the blind detective in the movie The Hidden Eye?

53

The Screen Actors Guild voted to give him an Oscar for special services, and he won a second Oscar for Best Supporting Actor. Identify this actor who gave a memorable performance in The Best Years of Our Lives.

54

In what 1941 film does James Cagney portray the role of Biff Grimes?

55

When Arsenic and Old Lace was filmed, Boris Karloff was unable to appear in his original stage role. Who replaced him?

56

In the film *High Sierra*, Humphrey Bogart's affections were torn between two women, a crippled girl he befriends and his "Moll." Who were his two female co-stars?

57

In what film did Bette Davis play Monty Woolley's secretary?

58

Name the Academy Award–winning song from the 1946 movie *The Harvey Girls*, starring Judy Garland, Ray Bolger, John Hodiak, and Angela Lansbury.

59

Gene Kelly made his screen debut as Judy Garland's co-star in what movie?

60

What was the title of Abbott and Costello's first movie?

61

In what movie did the screen characters Ma and Pa Kettle first appear? Who played the roles?

62

Who were the two stars in *The Major and Minor*?

63

Dan Dailey was nominated for the Best Actor in *When My Baby Smiles at Me*. To whom did he lose that Oscar?

64

Name the song that Kate Smith sang in the movie *This Is the Army*, which starred George Murphy, Joan Leslie, George Tobias, Alan Hale, and Ronald Reagan.

65

Name the musical, adapted from a 1944 Broadway show, that starred Gene Kelly, Frank Sinatra, Vera-Ellen, Betty Garrett, Ann Miller, and Jules Munchin.

66

In what motion picture did Burt Lancaster make his debut? The film starred Ava Gardner.

Clark Gable and Lana Turner

67

Vera-Ellen portrayed Miss Subways in what film?

68

Name the married couple who starred in the 1940 movie *I Want a Divorce*.

69

Nelson Eddy was teamed with what singer in the movie *The Chocolate Soldier?*

70

Name the stars who got married during the filming of *That Hamilton Lady*.

71

Margaret O'Brien discovered a magical, secluded garden in *The Secret Garden*. Who helped her?

72

In what movie does Frank Sinatra sing "Time after Time"?

73

What role did Scotty Beckett play in the movie *The Jolson Story*?

74

In her movie debut, Jennifer Jones won the Oscar for Best Actress in what film?

75

What actress said to Dooley Wilson in *Casablanca*: "Play it, Sam. Play 'As Time Goes By' "?

76

Who played opposite Margo in the acclaimed thriller *The Leopard Man*?

77

Who played Judge Roy Bean in *The Law West of Pecos*?

78

Who won the Oscar as Best Actor in a 1948 Shakespeare drama?

79

The following year, 1949, Broderick Crawford won the Best Actor Academy Award for what film?

80

"Here's looking at you kid" is a line from what 1943 movie?

81

What was Humphrey Bogart's character's name in *Casablanca*?

82

Name the star nominated for an Academy Award as Best Actress for her role in the movie Our Town.

83

Orson Welles's *Macbeth* co-starred what actress in the role as Lady Macbeth?

84

Who was known as "The Yodeling Comedienne"? (She appeared in the movie *Chatterbox*, with Joe E. Brown.)

85

What 1941 movie starred Bing Crosby, Carolyn Lee, and Eddie "Rochester" Anderson, and featured music like "St. Louis Blues," "St. James Infirmary," and "Melancholy Baby"?

86

Who played the title role of Ali Baba in the 1944 movie *Ali Baba and the Forty Thieves*?

87

Further to Question 86, who played Ali as a boy?

88

Name the New York City hotel where Gene Tierney first meets Clifton Webb in the movie *Laura*.

a) The Ritz Hotel
b) The Algonquin Hotel
c) The Mayflower Hotel
d) The Gold Crest Hotel

89

Lauren Bacall made her screen debut at the age of nineteen opposite Humphrey Bogart in what movie?

90

Name Charlie Chaplin's first talkie, which he also directed.

91

This actress starred in *Ziegfeld Girl*, *Peyton Place*, and *Imitation of Life*. She is:

a) Bette Davis
b) Jane Russell
c) Lana Turner
d) Maggie McNamara

Charlie Chaplin and Virginia Cherill

92

What movie marked Tony Curtis's film debut, and what stage name did he use then?

93

In what movie opposite Jack Benny does Margaret Dumont play Miss Rodholder?

94

Who portrayed the title role in the movie *Lillian Russell*?

95

Name the film biography of Marilyn Miller, starring June Haver.

96

What actress starred in *Gaslight*?

   a) Bette Davis
   b) Ingrid Bergman
   c) Joan Crawford

97

Jack Lemmon pursued writer Betty Garrett in what movie musical?

98

Name Gary Cooper's hobo pal, the Colonel, in Meet John Doe.

99

Who played the lead in the motion picture Knickerbocker Holiday?

100

"I'll Get By" was the song featured in what MGM motion picture starring Irene Dunne and Spencer Tracy?

The 1950s

1

Who won the Oscar for Best Actor for the movie The Bridge on the River Kwai?

2

Susan Hayward played what real-life murderess in the movie I Want to Live?

3

Who produced The Greatest Show on Earth?

4

In The Seven Year Itch, what movie did Marilyn Monroe and Tom Ewell go to see?

5

Name the 1952 movie that starred Gary Cooper, Grace Kelly, Lloyd Bridges, and Lon Chaney.

6

Name the three top stars who made cameo appearances in Orson Welles's A Touch of Evil, which starred Charlton Heston, Janet Leigh, and Welles himself.

Orson Welles

7

For what 1957 film did Red Buttons win an Oscar for Best Supporting Actor?

8

Who won Best Supporting Actress for *Sayonara*?

9

Who co-starred with Laurence Olivier in *The Prince and the Showgirl*?

10

Who starred in the movie *Show Boat* with Howard Keel?

11

Who won the Best Actress Academy Award in 1958? For what movie?

12

What 1954 horror/sci-fi flick starred Julia Adams and Richard Dean?

13

Name the theme song for *High Noon*.

14

Name the movie that starred Marilyn Monroe, Betty Grable, and Lauren Bacall.

15

Who won the Best Actress Oscar for *A Streetcar Named Desire?*

a) Thelma Ritter
b) Marilyn Monroe
c) Vivien Leigh
d) Maureen O'Hara

16

Her performance in *Three Faces of Eve* earned her the best Actress Oscar. Name her.

Doris Day and Jimmy Cagney

17

In the movie *Calamity Jane*, Doris Day played the title role. Who played Wild Bill Hickok?

18

In what film did Sidney Poitier and Tony Curtis appear chained together?

19

In Alfred Hitchcock's *Rear Window*, who portrays the neighbor whom James Stewart suspects of murdering his wife?

20

Dance with Me Henry was the final movie this comedy team did together. Name them.

21

Who played Barbara Stanwyck's husband in the movie *Titanic*?

22

Name the movie that starred Alan Freed, Tuesday Weld, Teddy Randazzo, and The Chuckles, Frankie Lyman and the Teenagers, The Flamingos, Johnny Burnette, Lavern Baker, and The Moonglows.

23

What was the nickname of Captain Philip Frances Queeg in *Caine Mutiny*?

24

What actress won an Oscar in 1959 for the film *Room at the Top*?

25

Name the actress who had the title role in the Broadway production of *The Diary of Anne Frank* and starred in the films *The Cobweb* (1956), *Picnic* (1956), and *Stage Struck* (1958).

26

Who played the title role in the film *Hercules*?

27

Humphrey Bogart, Joan Bennett, Basil Rathbone, Aldo Ray, and Peter Ustinov starred together in what movie?

28

In what movie, starring Shelley Winters and Raymond Burr, does Frank Sinatra sing "That Old Black Magic"?

29

Name the two actors nominated for Best Supporting Actor for the same film in 1953. What was the film?

30

"You're just not couth" is a quote from what film that starred Judy Holliday and Broderick Crawford?

31

What actress co-starred with Danny Thomas in *The Jazz Singer*?

32

Name Elvis Presley's first movie.

33

What is the title of the motion picture musical that starred Kathryn Grayson, Ava Gardner, Howard Keel, Joey Brown, and Agnes Moorehead?

34

Name the muscular actor who starred as Tarzan in the 1950s and was a former fireman, cowboy, and lifeguard in addition to being married to Vera Miles.

35

Who played the child lead in *The Bad Seed*?

36

What 1957 movie brought Brigitte Bardot before the American public's eye?

37

In what film does Maggie McNamara's character say: "Men are usually so bored with virgins. I'm so glad you're not"?

38

Who won an Oscar for portraying Zapata's brother in the movie *Viva, Zapata!*?

39

Name the actress who won an Academy Award for her performance as Lola Delaney in *Come Back, Little Sheba*?

40

In what movie does Judy Holliday portray the character Billie Dawn?

41

Richard Widmark, Jack Palance, Robert Wagner, Karl Malden, Jack Webb, and Martin Milner starred in what war movie?

42

Name the director of *The Seven Year Itch*, which starred Marilyn Monroe.

43

What is the title of the movie that starred Bob Hope, Milly Vitale, George Tobias, Billie Gray, and James Cagney?

44

Who co-starred with Rita Hayworth in the movie *Miss Sadie Thompson*?

67

45

Anthony Perkins's screen debut was in what movie that starred Spencer Tracy, Jean Simmons, and Theresa Wright?

46

Who challenged James Dean to a game of chicken in *Rebel Without a Cause?*

47

Name the motion picture that starred Alan Ladd for which the theme song, "Mona Lisa," won an Oscar.

48

Who played the role of Jim Thorpe in the film *Jim Thorpe— All American?*

49

Name the director of *Anatomy of a Murder*, which starred James Stewart, Eve Arden, and George C. Scott.

50

In the movie *Three Little Words*, who portrayed songwriters Bert Kalmar and Harry Ruby?

51

Ruth Gordon's book *Years Ago* was the basis for what 1953 movie?

52

In the 1952 film *Limelight*, to whom does Charlie Chaplin say: "There's something about working the streets that I like. It's the tramp in me, I suppose"?

53

In what movie did Elizabeth Taylor portray Katharine Hepburn's daughter-in-law?

54

Who portrayed Emperor Anthony in the classic movie *Quo Vadis*?

Paulette Goddard and Charlie Chaplin

55

What two stars portrayed *David and Bathsheba*?

56

Name the two stars who portrayed *Solomon and Sheba*.

57

Name the actor who made his screen debut in the 1956 movie *Baby Doll*.

58

Kirk Douglas, James Mason, Paul Lukas, and Peter Lorre starred in what 1954 Disney fantasy adventure movie?

59

Identify the two leading actors from the movie Kim.

60

Name the character portrayed by James Dean in the movie *Rebel Without a Cause*.

61

Who was the first actress to play the role of *Gidget*, in the 1959 movie?

62

Grace Kelly won an Oscar in 1954 for Best Actress. Name the movie.

63

The song "Diamonds Are a Girl's Best Friend" comes from what movie starring Marilyn Monroe and Betty Grable?

64

In the movie *Houdini* with Tony Curtis, who played his wife?

65

Name the only movie Lou Costello made without his partner, Bud Abbott.

66

What was James Dean's real name? What 1951 movie was his first?

67

What was the title of the movie for which the Oscar-nominated song "The High and the Mighty" was featured?

68

The 1959 movie *For the First Time* was the last film for what great singer?

69

The song "Pete Kelly's Blues" is from what mid-50s picture?

70

In what film does Marlene Dietrich flash her scars to Charles Laughton and say: "Want to Kiss Me, Ducky"?

71

In the movie *River of No Return*, Marilyn Monroe sang "Bye-Bye-Blackbird." Who sang that song in the 1954 movie *The Eddie Cantor Story*?

72

The 1955 Oscar-nominated song "Unchained Melody" comes from what movie?

73

Kirk Douglas, Eleanor Parker, Horace McMahon, and William Bendix starred in what police movie?

74

Jerry Lewis and Shirley MacLaine end up together in what 1955 comedy film?

75

Michael Rennie, Patricia Neal, Hugh Marlow, Billy Gray, and Sam Jaffe starred in what science fiction motion picture?

76

In the 1954 movie *White Christmas*, Bing Crosby and Danny Kaye teamed up with what two actresses?

Bing Crosby

77

In 1959, who won the Academy Award for Best Actor?

a) Laurence Harvey, *Room at the Top*
b) Charlton Heston, *Ben Hur*
c) Jack Lemmon, *Some Like It Hot*
d) Paul Muni, *The Last Angry Man*
e) James Stewart, *Anatomy of a Murder*

78

Humphrey Bogart co-starred with Audrey Hepburn in what 1954 movie?

79

Judy Garland's big number "Get Happy" comes from what film with Gene Kelly?

80

Deborah Kerr portrays a spinster in *Separate Tables*. With whom does she fall in love?

81

Name the star of the 1957 movie *I Was a Teenage Werewolf*.

82

James Whitmore and Keenan Wynn played comic gangsters in what musical?

83

Name Tony Curtis's two female co-stars in *Flesh and Fury*.

84

Who played James Dean's father in *Rebel Without a Cause*?

85

Name the actress whose opening number, "Think Pink," was a show stopper in 1957's *Funny Face*.

86

Who won the Oscar for Best Supporting Actress as Alma in *From Here to Eternity*?

87

What was James Dean's last movie?

88

Frank Sinatra portrays a heel who is kept by an older woman, but he won't dump girlfriend Kim Novak in the 1957 movie *Pal Joey*. Name the star who plays the older actress.

89

The Best Actor Academy Award in 1951 went to:

   a) Humphrey Bogart, *African Queen*
   b) Marlon Brando, *A Streetcar Named Desire*
   c) Montgomery Clift, *A Place in the Sun*
   d) Arthur Kennedy, *Bright Victory*
   e) Fredric March, *Death of a Salesman*

90

In what film did Errol Flynn portray John Barrymore?

91

Ernest Borgnine won the Best Actor Oscar in 1955 for what movie?

92

What 1954 movie starred Tony Curtis, Natalie Wood, Henry Fonda, Lauren Bacall, and Stubby Kaye?

93

Marlon Brando sings "Luck Be a Lady Tonight" in what 1955 movie?

94

In what 1954 film did Judy Garland sing "The Man That Got Away"?

95

What TV personality portrayed Benny Goodman in the 1955 movie *The Benny Goodman Story*?

96

What North American location was used for the parting of the seas in the historic 1956 movie *The Ten Commandments*, with Charlton Heston?

97

Mario Lanza portrayed a famous singer in what 1951 movie?

Mickey Rooney and Judy Garland

98

Who played baby Moses in *The Ten Commandments*?

99

Name the film that starred Tom Ewell, Jayne Mansfield, Edmond O'Brien, and Julie London.

100

For what film was Grace Kelly nominated for Best Supporting Actress?

101

Texas Lady starred what Academy Award–winning actress?

102

What was the title of Betty Grable's final film?

103

Who played John Wayne's kidnapped niece in *The Searchers*?

The 1960s

1

"Shut up and deal" is the final line that Shirley MacLaine says to Jack Lemmon in what movie?

2

In Butterfield 8, to whom does Elizabeth Taylor say: "Mama, face it; I was the slut of all time"?

3

Who portrays the founder of psychoanalysis in John Huston's movie Freud?

4

Cliff Robertson played John F. Kennedy in what WWII movie?

5

Who won the Best Actor Award for My Fair Lady?

6

In the movie *Let's Make Love*, starring Marilyn Monroe, Yves Montand, Tony Randall, and Frankie Vaughn, what role did Bing Crosby play?

7

In 1968 Mel Brooks won an Oscar for his screenplay. Name the movie.

8

Name the movie that starred Doris Day, Stephen Boyd, Jimmy Durante, Martha Raye, and Dean Jagger?

9

In what movie does Tony Curtis play marine Ira Hayes?

10

Who portrayed gangster Abe Reles in the motion picture *Murder, Inc.*?

11

Name the actor who played the role of James Bond in *Casino Royale*.

Jimmy Durante

12

This actress played the old-lady neighbor in the movie *Rosemary's Baby*. Name her.

13

Who won the Academy Award for Best Supporting Actress for portraying Blanche Barrow in *Bonnie and Clyde*?

14

In Alfred Hitchcock's thriller *The Birds*, who played the schoolteacher attacked by the birds?

15

Judy Holliday's leading man in *Bells Are Ringing* was?

16

Who did former boxing champ Muhammad Ali portray in the 1966 movie *Requiem for a Heavyweight*?

17

In what movie does Barbra Streisand say: "That's where I live, on stage"?

18

Who played the role of Mama Rose in *Gypsy*?

19

Who played the role of the obscure university professor who rose to fame as a Broadway critic in the 1960 movie version of *Please Don't Eat the Daisies*?

20

What was the title of the movie, scripted by Harold Pinter, about an Oxford professor who falls in love with a student?

21

Name the 1961 rags-to-riches story that starred Susan Hayward and Dean Martin.

22

Who played the Bostonian butler who learns to fend for himself in The Adventures of Bullwhip Griffin, also starring Suzanne Pleshette?

23

Who played Huck in the 1960 version of The Adventures of Huckleberry Finn?

24

Charles Laughton's last film was a movie adaptation of an Allen Drury novel. What was the film's title?

25

What was the title of the tear-jerker starring William Holden that revealed the relationship between a young boy and his wealthy father?

26

What 1964 film made Clint Eastwood an international superstar and boosted the career of Sergio Leone as director?

27

What movie, starring Dick Van Dyke, marked the film debut of both Barbara Feldon and Sam Waterston?

28

In Five Miles to Midnight, Tony Perkins convinces his wife to collect insurance money when it is assumed he has been killed. Who played the wife?

29

In what film does Elvis Presley play a half-breed Indian who must choose sides when his mother's people go on the warpath?

30

The 1968 movie *Mrs. Brown, You've Got a Lovely Daughter* featured what musical group?

31

Name the title of the film that brings the Munsters, the family of the popular TV sitcom, to England to claim inheritance on a castle.

32

Who serves as narrator for *Night Gallery*, a three-story anthology starring Roddy McDowall and Joan Crawford?

33

What WWII whodunit stars Peter O'Toole and Omar Sharif?

34

What 1966 movie starred Michael Caine, Shelley Winters, Julia Foster, and Shirley Ann Field? (Hint: The hit song from the movie is the same as its title.)

35

Name Neil Simon's first play to reach the screen, which starred Frank Sinatra in 1963.

36

Dustin Hoffman starred in the movie *The Graduate*. What actor originally turned down the role?

37

In *The Great Impostor*, with Tony Curtis, who co-starred with him as Father Devlin?

38

Who won an Oscar for Best Supporting Actor for his role in Tennessee Williams's *Sweet Bird of Youth*, which starred Geraldine Page and Paul Newman?

39

What movie, based on a novel by Truman Capote, won an Oscar in 1961?

40

Who portrayed the role of Marion Crane in the 1960 Alfred Hitchcock movie *Psycho*?

41

Who played Uncle Albert, the man who loved to laugh, in Walt Disney's *Mary Poppins*?

42

Who did John Wayne portray in How the West Was Won?

43

Who directed the film The Fortune Cookie?

44

What was the Academy Award–winning movie for 1963?

a) How the West Was Won
b) Lilies of the Field
c) Cleopatra
d) Tom Jones

45

What film won the following three Oscars for Billy Wilder: Best Picture, Best Director, and Best Screenplay?

46

Marilyn Monroe and Jean Harlow both co-starred with Clark Gable in their last films. Can you name them?

Clark Gable and Jean Harlow

47

Who falls in love with Warren Beatty in *Splendor in the Grass*?

48

Who won Best Supporting Actor for his role as Jack Lemmon's brother-in-law in *The Fortune Cookie*?

49

Peter Ustinov won the first of his two Oscars for his role in what Stanley Kubrick film?

50

Who did Don Murray portray in *One Man's Way*?

51

Name the hooker with a heart of gold in the 1969 musical *Sweet Charity*.

52

What was the name of the character played by Rod Steiger in the 1965 movie *The Pawnbroker*?

53

What was Ernie Kovacs's last film (1961), which involves the robbery of a bank in Boston by ship?

54

What famous recording artist took a non-singing role in the 1960 movie Elmer Gantry, which starred Burt Lancaster and Jean Simmons?

55

What is the title of Robert Redford's first movie?

56

Who starred with Rod Taylor in Hitchcock's The Birds?

57

What actor made his film debut as Boo Radley in To Kill a Mockingbird?

58

What was the title of the unusual MGM animated feature, based on the Norton Juster book, that had Butch Patrick supplying a voice?

59

Which actor starred in *The Picasso Summer*, which was based on a Ray Bradbury story?

   a) Roddy McDowall
   b) William Holden
   c) Hal Holbrook
   d) Albert Finney
   e) Robert York

60

Name the film that featured Nancy Sinatra as a tax inspector and Elvis Presley as a stockcar racer.

61

Who portrayed the role of a drunken mother in *From the Terrace*, with Paul Newman and Joanne Woodward?

62

Who played the sinister spy in *From Russia with Love*, with Sean Connery?

63

Who directed *The Great Race*, with Tony Curtis, Natalie Wood, Jack Lemmon, and Peter Falk?

64

What 1966 Disney film, starring Fred MacMurray, Vera Miles, and Lillian Gish, had a small town starting a Boy Scout troop?

65

What 1962 film has Elvis Presley singing "Home Is Where the Heart Is" and "On Top of Old Smokey"?

66

What actor quits college to become a champion sports-car racer in *The Lively Set*?

67

What comedy, based on a Tennessee Williams play, starred Tony Franciosa, Jane Fonda, Jim Hutton, and Lois Nettleton?

68

Identify the movie, with Nigel Patrick, Yvonne Mitchell, and Aldo Ray, in which an Irish priest suspects murder when a drunken author is killed.

69

Who played Oliver Reed's brother in *The Jokers*?

70

What movie is the first of four films to star Margaret Rutherford as Agatha Christie's character Miss Marple?

71

What 1962 film included the musical scores "76 Trombones," "Till There Was You," and "Trouble"?

72

Who starred in *The President's Analyst*?

73

In what 1960 film does actor John Ericson play the role of a 1930s gangster?

74

What comedy, based on Nathaniel Benchley's novel *The Off-Islanders*, served as the film debut for Alan Arkin?

75

Who plays the wife shared by Clint Eastwood and Lee Marvin in *Paint Your Wagon*?

- a) Jane Fonda
- b) Jean Seberg
- c) Cloris Leachman
- d) Beverly Todd
- e) Susannah York

76

Name the 1967 film with seven episodes of Shirley Mac-Laine showing seven kinds of women.

77

Who served as narrator for The World of Abbott and Costello?

78

What martial-arts expert exchanges one line of dialogue with the character of Matt Helm in The Wrecking Crew, starring Dean Martin, Sharon Tate, and Elke Sommer?

79

Name Montgomery Clift's last movie, which features a cameo appearance by Roddy McDowall.

80

Excluding his early nudie, Tonight for Sure, what film was Francis Ford Coppola's directorial debut?

81

Which actor starred in Desire in the Dust:

    a) Montgomery Clift
    b) Richard Burton
    c) James Mason
    d) Gregory Peck
    e) Raymond Burr

Bud Abbott and Lou Costello

82

What 1969 movie, starring Vince Edwards as head of a psychiatric telephone service, later became a short-lived TV series called *Matt Lincoln*?

83

What actor starred in *Diary of a Madman*, a story of a nineteenth-century magistrate possessed by an evil spirit that compels him to murder?

84

What comedienne co-stars with Bob Denver in a 1968 movie about a traveling saleslady?

85

In *Die, Monster, Die!*, what out-of-this-world object does Boris Karloff discover that gives him strange powers?

86

What 1967 musical, starring Rex Harrison, earned an Academy Award for its special visual effects?

87

What film, starring Vincent Price, was the first of Roger Corman's eight Edgar Allan Poe film adaptations?

88

In *How to Murder Your Wife*, Jack Lemmon marries what actress while he's drunk?

89

Who plays the detective in *It's a Mad Mad Mad Mad World*?

90

In what 1969 film does Charlton Heston play a New Orleans Saints quarterback?

91

In *The Art of Love*, name the actor who plays a struggling artist in France who fakes death to increase the value of his work.

92

For what movie were theater patrons given "ghost viewers" to enable them to see the spirits?

93

What was the name of the hotel run by Anthony Perkins in Alfred Hitchcock's notorious classic *Psycho*?

94

In what film, starring Joanne Woodward, did Paul Newman make his directorial debut?

95

Two dogs and a cat make a 250-mile trek across Canada to be with their family of humans. Name the movie.

96

What musical group appears in Woody Allen's redubbed movie *What's Up, Tiger Lily?*

97

Alistair MacLean's novel *Where Eagles Dare* was made into a film that starred what two actors?

98

Elizabeth Taylor and Sandy Dennis won Oscars for what film directed by Mike Nichols, which also starred Richard Burton?

99

The cartoon *Gay Purr-ee* featured the voices of Robert Goulet and what actress?

   a) Barbra Streisand
   b) Lillian Gish
   c) Judy Garland
   d) Sophia Loren
   e) Zsa Zsa Gabor

100

What was the first major rock-concert film shot in 1967? (It featured Janis Joplin, The Who, Jimi Hendrix, and the Jefferson Airplane.)

105

The 1970s

1

In the *Poseidon Adventure*, to whom is Shelley Winters married?

2

Who co-stars with Liza Minnelli as her bisexual lover in *Cabaret*?

3

The Game of Death was the ironic title of the last movie for what actor?

4

Actor Larry Hagman directed only one movie in 1972. It was a sequel to a horror film. Name the movie.

5

What actor portrayed Judge Roy Bean, the hanging judge?

6

In what film does Vincent Price, disfigured in a car accident, seek revenge on those responsible for the death of his wife?

7

In what film does Bernadette Peters make her debut? (It starred Cliff Robertson and was written by Steven Spielberg.)

8

Who played a con man in *Adios Amigo*, an offbeat Western comedy written, directed, and produced by Fred Williamson?

9

What film, starring Warren Oates and Ben Johnson, depicts the life of a notorious gangster shot down outside the Biograph Theater?

10

In I Love You, *Goodbye*, a frustrated suburban housewife leaves her family to make it on her own. Who starred in the film?

11

Who directed Taxi Driver, with Robert De Niro, Cybill Shepherd, and a memorable performance by Jodi Foster?

12

In The Teacher, what actor and actress have cameo appearances as disapproving bystanders in a restaurant scene?

13

What movie, starring Sid Caesar, Imogene Coca, and Carl Reiner displays ten skits as spoofs on classic films? (The skits include a spoof on From Here to Eternity and This Is Your Life.)

14

What well-known country singer makes his acting debut in A Gunfight?

15

Who gave a brilliant performance as the Scarecrow in the 1978 musical The Wiz?

W. C. Fields

16

Name the demented doctor who created Humanimals—creatures half man, half beast—in the horror/fantasy thriller The Island of Dr. Moreau?

17

What kind of handicapped children does Diane Keaton teach in her role as Theresa Dunn in Looking for Mr. Goodbar?

18

What musical group provides the odd electronic musical score for the 1977 movie Sorcerer?

19

Identify the 1978 space thriller whose cast includes Elliott Gould, James Brolin, Hal Holbrook, Sam Waterston, Karen Black, and O. J. Simpson?

20

Burt Reynolds made his directing debut in what film?

21

In *Mary, Queen of Scots*, Vanessa Redgrave plays Mary. Who plays Queen Elizabeth?

a) Bette Davis
b) Debbie Reynolds
c) Lynn Redgrave
d) Glenda Jackson
e) Diane Keaton

22

Who won the Best Screenplay Oscar for the 1970s movie M*A*S*H?

23

Who starred as the former high-school athlete who discovers that life is more difficult than being on the playing field in the film *Rabbit Run*?

24

What 1975 hit movie, starring Roy Scheider and Robert Shaw, earned three Oscars and was followed by three sequels?

25

Name the movie, starring Ellen Burstyn and Kris Kristoffer-son, that later became the basis for the long-running TV sitcom "Alice."

26

What 1979 space-age horror film, starring Sigourney Weaver and Tom Skerrit, had a famous dinner scene in which a creature emerged from the stomach of a human?

27

In what 1975 movie do Elliott Gould and Julie Christie play themselves?

28

Who played the troubled priest who attempts to con-quer the demon that is possessing Linda Blair in The Exorcist?

29

In *Corvette Summer*, Mark Hamill falls for a hooker in Las Vegas. Who plays the prostitute?

30

What Monty Python film has the crew on a medieval crusade?

31

Bernard Lee makes his last appearance as M in what 1979 James Bond film?

32

Director Steve Ihnat died shortly after making what film about an aging rodeo performer, which starred James Coburn and Lois Nettleton?

33

Who sings the National Anthem in *Two Minute Warning*, with Charlton Heston and John Cassavetes?

34

Who played the leading female role in Being There, with Peter Sellers and Melvyn Douglas?

a) Shirley MacLaine
b) Lucille Ball
c) Jacqueline Bisset
d) Catherine Deneuve
e) Elizabeth Hartman

35

What 1979 Woody Allen film, involving a comedy writer and his friends, was photographed in black and white and Panavision?

36

Who plays Bette Midler's manager in The Rose?

37

Name the 1976 film that won an Oscar for its visual effects, in which people become extinct at age thirty?

Lucille Ball

38

Lauren Bacall was one of the suspects in what Agatha Christie mystery film?

39

John Wayne and Lauren Bacall starred in what Western drama in 1976?

40

Name the male actor who co-starred with Diana Ross in the 1972 film *Lady Sings the Blues*?

41

Clint Eastwood portrayed *Dirty Harry* in the movies, but what was Harry's last name?

42

Who won the 1976 Best Supporting Actor Oscar as the hard-hitting editor in *All the President's Men*?

43

Liza Minnelli won an Oscar in 1972 for Best Actress. Name the movie.

44

Who provided the voice of Charlotte in *Charlotte's Web*?

45

Fay Wray played King Kong's romantic interest in the 1933 movie. Who played the same role in the 1976 remake?

46

In what 1974 movie did acting coach Lee Strasberg make his screen debut? (His student Al Pacino starred in the film.)

47

Who played Jack Lemmon's wife in *The Prisoner of 2nd Avenue*?

48

In 1970 and 1972, two actors refused to accept their Oscars for Best Actor. Name the actors. Name the films.

49

Name the last movie Marlene Dietrich made (1979), which starred Kim Novak, David Bowie, Maria Schell, and Curt Jurgens.

50

Name the actress nominated for Best Supporting Actress in the 1970 movie M*A*S*H. (She portrayed Major Houlihan.)

51

What actress starred with Charles Bronson in the 1974 motion picture Death Wish?

52

In the 1978 film version of Superman, Christopher Reeve plays the man of steel. Who plays Lois Lane?

53

What film stars Jack Nicholson as a musician with great promise who abandons his career to work on an oil rig?

54

What actor and actress played the leading roles in *Love Story*?

55

What 1971 film, starring Topol, earned Oscars for cinematography and musical scoring?

56

What state is the setting for the beautifully photographed black-and-white film *The Last Picture Show*?

57

In what movie, with Jack Nicholson, Candice Bergen, and Ann-Margret, did Carol Kane make her film debut?

58

What British rock group appeared in Tommy, with Ann-Margret and Oliver Reed?

59

Name the actor who makes his directorial debut for Kotch, starring Walter Matthau.

60

Who played the character of Alix in Stanley Kubrick's A Clockwork Orange?

61

What 1971 movie, starring Gene Hackman and Roy Scheider, earned five Oscars?

62

Name the actor who stuffed cotton in his mouth to play the role of Don Corleone in The Godfather.

63

James Dickey, author of the novel *Deliverance*, appears in the film adaptation of his book as what character?

64

Who makes her acting debut as Billie Holiday in *Lady Sings the Blues*?

65

In what 1972 film does Laurence Olivier lead his wife's lover, played by Michael Caine, into a diabolical trap?

66

Who directed the highly controversial film *Last Tango in Paris*?

67

What is the title of the movie, based on Stephen King's novel, that deals with vampirism in a small New England town?

123

68

Tatum O'Neal's film debut earned her an Oscar. Name the movie, which also starred her father, Ryan O'Neal.

69

What 1973 film, directed by George Lucas, propelled Richard Dreyfuss to stardom?

70

In the movie *Serpico*, who plays the role of an undercover cop who exposes corruption in the New York City police force?

71

Who plays the political activist in *The Way We Were*?

72

In *The Exorcist*, who supplies the voice of the devil that emanates from the on-screen mouth of fourteen-year-old Linda Blair?

- a) Louise Fletcher
- b) Joanne Woodward
- c) Ellen Burstyn
- d) Glenda Jackson
- e) Mercedes McCambridge

73

What 1973 movie, starring Robert De Niro and Harvey Keitel, brought director Martin Scorsese mass recognition?

74

Name the Woody Allen comedy that tells the tale of a man who is frozen in 1973 and awakens two hundred years later.

75

In the 1974 film adaptation of F. Scott Fitzgerald's *The Great Gatsby*, Robert Redford played the title role, and Mia Farrow played Daisy Buchanan. Who played the hit-and-run victim Myrtle Wilson?

76

Name the director of Chinatown who appears briefly as the hood who knifes Jack Nicholson.

77

Name the 1974 film, starring Steve McQueen, Paul Newman, William Holden, Faye Dunaway, and Fred Astaire, that won an Oscar for cinematography?

78

Who played the Acid Queen in the rock opera Tommy?

79

Who designed the twenty-five gowns worn by Diana Ross in Mahogany?

80

What New York City punk group performs "Teenage Lobotomy" and "I Wanna Be Sedated" in Rock 'n' Roll High School?

81

Who plays Sylvester Stallone's shy girlfriend in the 1976 blockbuster Rocky?

82

What film, directed by George Lucas, made R2D2 a household word?

83

Mikhail Baryshnikov made his film debut in what film?

84

What 1977 film about UFOs is Columbia Pictures most profitable movie to date?

85

Who plays the Brooklyn youth in Saturday Night Fever who finds meaning in his life only while dancing at a disco?

86

Name the title of Warren Beatty's remake of Here Comes Mr. Jordan.

127

87

Who plays the poor Southern textile worker in *Norma Rae?*

88

A nuclear power plant on Three Mile Island, Pennsylvania, leaked radioactive steam into the atmosphere. This incident occurred two weeks after the premiere of what movie that deals with a nuclear plant's spillage?

89

Who plays Woody Allen's faithful, seventeen-year-old girl-friend in the black-and-white movie *Manhattan?*

90

What movie shows Martin Sheen as a special agent who journeys up the river in Cambodia with orders to locate and kill Marlon Brando?

91

Name the 1979 German film, based on the book by Gunter Grass, that won a Best Foreign Film Academy Award.

92

What movie, about director Bob Fosse, includes a memorable scene showing open-heart surgery? (A New York City hospital surgical team was enlisted to add realism to this graphic scene.)

93

In the famous breakfast scene in *Kramer vs. Kramer*, what is Dustin Hoffman teaching his son to cook?

94

Who plays the veteran horsetrainer in the 1979 film *The Black Stallion*?

a) Alan Alda
b) Mickey Rooney
c) Bing Crosby
d) Linda Blair
e) Harrison Ford

95

What 1978 smash success has a gay couple trying to act straight for the sake of Ugo Tognazzi's son?

96

Who directed Sean Connery and Michael Caine in *The Man Who Would Be King*?

129

Gloria Jean and Bing Crosby

97

What odd 1974 film has a couple attempting to escape the rat race by turning into a tree?

98

Who played Dracula in the 1979 version, which also starred Laurence Olivier?

99

In what film did Meryl Streep make her acting debut?

100

Who plays the beer-guzzling coach of a hopeless little league baseball team with female star pitcher Tatum O'Neal in *The Bad News Bears*?

The 1980s

1

The Hunter was what star's final film?

2

Who was the only pro wrestler to play himself in the film Micki and Maude, which starred Dudley Moore and Amy Irving?

3

Whose voice did Jessica Lange lip sync to in the movie Sweet Dreams?

4

In the humorous restaurant scene in Splash, what did Daryl Hannah eat?

5

Name the multi-million-dollar scare comedy that has Bill Murray and Dan Aykroyd getting "slimed" by ghosts.

6

Who played Jack Nicholson's wife in The Shining?

7

What outrageous punk rock group is featured in *The Great Rock and Roll Swindle*?

8

Who played the deranged psychiatrist in the film *Hairspray*, directed by John Waters?

9

In *Half Moon Street*, Sigourney Weaver plays a Ph.D. researcher by day and a call girl by night. Who plays the British diplomat with whom she becomes involved?

a) Mel Gibson
b) Bryan Brown
c) Michael Caine
d) Richard Gere
e) James Woods

10

Who directed *The Hand*, in which the drawing hand of a cartoonist is severed in a car accident and then goes on a murder spree?

135

11

In what movie did film star Eddie Murphy make his debut as a writer and director.

12

At what age did Danny DeVito and Arnold Schwarzenegger discover they were twins?

13

Who starred and sang in the Loretta Lynn story, *Coal Miner's Daughter*?

14

In the film *Ordinary People*, what kind of accident took the life of Timothy Hutton's brother?

15

What was the real name of the Elephant Man?

16

Who appeared on screen as the flamboyant director in 1980s *The Stunt Man*?

17

In what movie does Goldie Hawn play a naive Jewish-American Princess who enlists in the army and finds self-confidence?

18

Who won an Academy Award for his starring role in *Raging Bull*?

19

What was Henry Fonda's last feature film?

20

Who won the Best Supporting Actress Academy Award for her performance in *Reds*?

21

What 1982 film, starring Jack Lemmon and Sissy Spacek, deals with the disappearance of Ed Horman and prompted the U.S. government to release a three-page statement denying that it failed "to act effectively" regarding Horman's murder?

137

22

In *Victor/Victoria*, who plays a down-and-out singer in the 1930s who is talked into masquerading as a man who is pretending to be a woman in a Paris cabaret?

23

Who plays the tough drill instructor in *An Officer and a Gentleman*?

24

What Steven Spielberg film has an alien riding on a bicycle?

25

Who played Paul Newman's courtroom adversary in *The Verdict*?

26

What two languages did Meryl Streep have to master for her role in *Sophie's Choice*?

27

In order to play the title role in *Gandhi*, what actor prepared himself by meditating in his hotel room, surrounded by photographs of Mahatma?

28

In *The World According to Garp*, who played the transexual ex-football player Robert Muldoon?

29

Who made her feature film debut as Garp's mother in *The World According to Garp*?

30

What 1981 West German film was nominated for six Academy Awards—the most for a foreign language movie?

31

What film has its characters reuniting for the funeral of a friend?

32

In what movie does iconoclastic test pilot Chuck Yeager have a cameo role as a bartender?

33

In order to play the role of *Playboy* playmate Dorothy Stratten, what actress increased her bust size by having plastic surgery?

34

Who played Shirley MacLaine's lecherous, potbellied neighbor in *Terms of Endearment*?

35

Who played Meryl Streep's lesbian housemate in *Silkwood*?

36

What was the title of Barbra Streisand's musical version of an Isaac Bashevis Singer short story?

37

Who played the effeminate assistant to Albert Finney in *The Dresser*?

38

In *Greystoke: The Legend of Tarzan, Lord of the Apes*, leading lady Andy MacDowell's voice was dubbed by whom?

Barbra Streisand

39

What was the name of the cow belonging to Sissy Spacek and Mel Gibson in *The River*?

40

Who won the Best Actress Oscar for her performance in *Places in the Heart*?

41

In the film *Amadeus*, name the actor whose performance as the composer Salieri won him an Oscar.

42

Who won the Oscar for Best Supporting Actress in 1984 for her performance as Mrs. Moore in *A Passage to India*?

   a) Glenn Close
   b) Peggy Ashcroft
   c) Lindsay Wagner
   d) Amy Irving
   e) Meryl Streep

43

What movie, starring Harrison Ford, prompted the National Committee for Amish Religious Freedom to lead a boycott against the film?

44

What was the name of the teenage boy in *Mask* whose face had been disfigured by a rare disease?

45

Name the film in which a gay man and a political activist are locked together in a South American prison.

46

Who received rave reviews for her portrayal of a Brooklyn Mafia princess in *Prizzi's Honor*?

47

By flipping television channels in his hotel room, Quincy Jones, co-producer of *The Color Purple*, discovered the actress to play the role of Whoopi Goldberg's strong-willed step-daughter for the film. Who was this first-time actress?

48

Name the film in which Mia Farrow's real-life mother, Maureen O'Sullivan, and Farrow's seven children had small parts.

49

In *Aliens*, Sigourney Weaver reprised her role as what gun-carrying warrior?

50

What film, directed by David Lynch, begins with a close-up of ants crawling on a detached human ear?

51

Who plays Paul Newman's sidekick in *The Color of Money*?

52

Name the actress who won an Oscar for her role as a deaf janitor in *Children of a Lesser God*?

53

Name the director of *Peggy Sue Got Married*.

a) Jonathan Demme
b) Penny Marshall
c) David Lynch
d) Ron Howard
e) Francis Ford Coppola

54

Who played the three Southern sisters in *Crimes of the Heart*?

55

What war is the setting for the Oliver Stone–directed movie *Platoon*?

56

What role does Jack Nicholson play in *The Witches of Eastwick*?

57

Name the movie, based upon a very successful TV series, that told how a federal agent battled the underworld and police corruption in Chicago during prohibition.

58

In *Fatal Attraction*, what did Anne Archer find cooking in the pot on her stove?

59

Who plays the blind sister to Lillian Gish in 1987's *The Whales of August*?

60

It took two years of negotiations with the People's Republic of China before Bertolucci could film on location there. Name the movie.

61

Empire of the Sun is adapted from the autobiographical novel by J. G. Ballard. In what early scene in the movie does Ballard appear?

146

Bette Davis

62

What movie, starring Michael Douglas, was aided by the October 19, 1987, stock market crash that occurred two months before its release?

63

Name the film, starring William Hurt, that Dan Rather called "an appropriate warning about the dangers of whom you put on the air."

64

Who plays the juror who helps Cher, a public defender, battle a practically hopeless case?

65

Who plays Cher's philosophical mother in *Moonstruck*?

66

Because of her role in *Fatal Attraction*, who was labeled by a supermarket tabloid as "The Most Hated Woman in America"?

67

Who played the role of Adrian Cronauer, a colorful army disc jockey in Saigon in the movie *Good Morning Vietnam*?

68

Name the film that starred Steve Martin in an updated version of *Cyrano de Bergerac*.

69

Name the film that has Robin Williams urging his students to "Seize the day."

70

Based on a James Joyce short story, what was the last movie directed by John Huston?

71

What film chronicles John Boorman's experience of living through the London air raids during WWII?

72

Who directed the 1987 film *Full Metal Jacket*?

  a) Stanley Kubrick
  b) Francis Ford Coppola
  c) Oliver Stone
  d) John Boorman
  e) Norman Jewison

73

Who served as narrator for the 1987 movie *Radio Days*?

74

In *My Left Foot*, Daniel Day-Lewis portrays Christie Brown, a fiesty Irish artist/writer. From what disease did he suffer?

75

What country is the setting for the poignant comedy *My Life as a Dog*?

76

Name the movie, directed by James Ivory, that shows how a young British man comes to terms with his homosexuality in the early 1900s.

150

77

In *Raising Arizona*, what actor and actress play a couple who kidnap one of a set of quintuplets because they can't have a child of their own?

78

Who played the dying police officer who is transformed into an ultra-sophisticated cyborg and seeks revenge on those who killed him?

79

In *The River's Edge*, name the biker who can't relate to a group of teenagers after one of their clique is murdered?

80

In *Ladyhawke*, Michelle Pfeiffer turns into a hawk by day, but what is Rutger Hauer transformed into by night?

81

What 1989 hit movie has Michelle Pfeiffer lying atop a piano while singing "Making Whoopee"?

82

In *Class*, who plays the beautiful older woman with whom Andrew McCarthy has an affair, only to discover she is the mother of his prep-school buddy?

83

Name the movie, starring Daryl Hannah, that uses subtitles to translate the primitive tongue of a group of nomadic Neanderthals?

84

In the 1986 remake of *The Fly*, who plays the scientist who tests himself in a genetic machine and begins to evolve into a human fly?

85

Who plays the reckless undercover cop partnered with Danny Glover in *Lethal Weapon*?

86

Name the 1986 film in which Gary Oldman plays the bass player for the punk rock group The Sex Pistols and Chloe Webb plays the American girlfriend he murders.

87

What California-locale film stars Nick Nolte, Richard Dreyfuss, and Bette Midler, and has a special appearance by Little Richard?

88

Who stars in *Captain Eo*, a short film shown only at California's Disneyland and Florida's Epcot Center?

89

Name the movie for which Chris Menges won an Oscar for cinematography, which tells the story of a Jesuit mission in the jungles of Brazil in the late-eighteenth century. (The movie stars Robert De Niro and Jeremy Irons.)

90

In *Road House*, Patrick Swayze plays the role of an NYU college graduate who prefers being a bouncer at a small-town bar. What was his major in school?

91

Who plays a sleek restaurant owner in *Tequila Sunrise*?

92

What was the make of the car that transported Michael J. Fox in *Back to the Future*?

93

Who directed the 1985 box office hit *Cocoon*?

a) Oliver Stone
b) Ron Howard
c) Rick Rosenthal
d) Roger Donaldson
e) Penny Marshall

94

Who was the real-life anthropologist that Sigourney Weaver portrays in *Gorillas in the Mist*?

95

Who played the leading male role in *The Cotton Club*? He even played his own cornet solos.

96

Who portrayed the minister of a town where dancing had been outlawed in *Footloose?*

97

In what film does Jennifer Beals play a construction welder by day and a sexy dancer by night?

98

In *The Best Little Whorehouse in Texas,* who plays the town's sheriff who tries to prevent the closing of the Chicken Ranch, a popular sporting house run by Dolly Parton?

99

In *Roadie,* who is the rock star who Meat Loaf and Kaki Hunter are trying to meet?

100

Can you name the movie that covers sixty years of Chinese history, used nineteen thousand extras, nine thousand costumes, and four different actors in the title role?

The 1990s

1

In *Ghost*, Patrick Swayze is unable to tell Demi Moore that he loves her. So when she says "I love you," what is his one-word response?

2

Who plays the L.A. cop who is tracking down the spirit of a deceased devil follower in *The First Power*?

3

Name the male and female stars of the 1990 film *Bird on a Wire*.

4

The Repossessed, starring Linda Blair, is a spoof on what 1970s hit movie?

5

Who stars as the Soviet submarine captain who is planning to defect to the United States?

6

Who plays the flaky nurse in Men Don't Leave?

7

In Men at Work, what is the profession of Charlie Sheen and Emilio Estevez?

8

Who plays the brave and sassy Linda Voss in Shining Through, with Michael Douglas?

9

In Mambo Kings, who plays the role of Desi Arnaz?

10

Name the film with Keifer Sutherland and Julia Roberts about medical students experimenting with life after death?

11

Who plays the small-town doctor who is afraid of spiders in Arachnophobia?

12

In *Basic Instincts*, who portrays the author of murder mysteries that have a way of predicting actual crimes?

13

Name the writer and director of *Shadows and Fog*, with John Malkovich and Jodie Foster.

14

Name the handyman for the Bartel family in *The Hand That Rocks the Cradle*.

15

Who plays the middle-age executive who is really Peter Pan at heart in *Hook*?

16

In *Ghost*, whose unscrupulous actions bring Patrick Swayze back from the dead in pursuit of revenge?

17

Name the two female stars of *Thelma and Louise*.

18

Identify the controversial standup comic who stars in *The Adventures of Ford Fairlane*.

19

In *Air America*, two airplane pilots are part of the CIA's smuggling operation in Laos during the Vietnam War. Can you name the stars who played the roles?

20

In *Another 48 Hours*, name the actor who helps detective Nick Nolte solve a case and save his police career.

21

Michael J. Fox is transported to what time period in *Back to the Future II*?

22

Name the 1990 film in which James Spader befriends Rob Lowe after Lowe gets him out of a barroom confrontation.

23

What Western, about three men who purchase Billy the Kid's horse, served as John Clark Gable's (Gable's son) screen debut?

24

Who played the role of the bride in Betsy's Wedding?

25

What former cancan dancer at the 1964 World's Fair, went on to play a leading role in House Sitter?

26

Name the starring actor in the film The Blood of Heroes.

27

Who plays the psycho killer who stalks Jamie Lee Curtis in *Blue Steel*?

28

Who plays Tinkerbell in *Hook*?

29

Who plays the pregnant teenager in *She's Having a Baby*?

30

Name the movie that contains a memorable scene in which a hand that has been shot off is carried away by a dog, while the hand's original owner is frantically looking for it so he can have it sewn back on.

31

Who played Kurt Russell's younger brother in *Backdraft*?

32

Who died in bed after making love to Kristie Alley in *Sibling Rivalry?*

33

Name the two actors who played nuns in *Nuns on the Run.*

34

Who had a romantic interest in Tom Hanks in *Joe Versus the Volcano?*

35

In *The Freshman*, who played the role satirizing Marlon Brando's role in *The Godfather?*

36

Who had the leading male role in *Love at Large?*

37

Who is the first patient awakened by Robin Williams in *Awakenings*?

38

Who directed the film *Backdraft*?

a) Oliver Stone
b) Jonathan Demme
c) John Singleton
d) Glenn Jordan
e) Ron Howard

39

Name the radio personality in *Pump Up the Volume*.

40

In the romantic adventure *Revenge*, what two actors are at odds?

165

41

Name the 1991 film starring Wesley Snipes and rapper Ice-T.

42

In *Three Men and a Little Lady*, who is reprimanded for teaching a child to say "What a crock"?

43

Who plays the leading role in *State of Grace*?

a) Mickey Rourke
b) Sean Penn
c) Alec Baldwin
d) Peter Strauss
e) Jason Patric

44

Name the two former "Saturday Night Live" players featured in the 1991 comedy *Nothing but Trouble*.

166

45

In what movie do Ray Liotta and Robert De Niro play men involved in organized crime?

46

In Green Card, what country does Gerard Depardieu come from?

47

Who plays Sylvester Stallone's butler in the 1991 film Oscar?

48

Who stars in the 1990 film Opportunity Knocks?

49

Name Dudley Moore's profession before he is committed to a mental hospital in Crazy People.

50

Who plays Sylvester Stallone's mother in *Stop! Or My Mom Will Shoot?*

51

Who plays the good cop in *One Good Cop?*

52

In *Pretty Woman*, who plays the star hooker?

53

Name the futuristic film starring Anthony Quinn and Emilio Estevez in which a man's head can house another man's mind.

54

Who made her directorial debut with *Little Man Tate?*

55

Who plays the clairvoyant in *The Butcher's Wife*?

56

Name the film in which Jeff Bridges, an unemployed disc jockey, is saved by Robin Williams, a homeless man searching for the Holy Grail.

57

During the first evening she spends with Richard Gere, what TV sitcom is Julia Roberts watching in *Pretty Woman*?

58

Name the sequel to Tom Clancy's *The Hunt for Red October*.

59

Who plays the bride's father in *Betsy's Wedding*?

60

What's the name of Joe Pesci's character in *Lethal Weapon III*?

61

Name the leading male and female roles in *Far and Away*.

62

Who portrays Jamie Lee Curtis's mother in *Blue Steel*?

63

Who betrays Goldie Hawn in *Deceived*?

64

Who has the part of Dillon, the spiritual leader, in *Alien 3*?

65

In *Encino Man*, what does Pauly Shore discover in his back-yard?

66

Why are the actors in *Alien 3* bald?

67

What Ron Howard movie is filmed in 70mm?

68

Who plays Gomez in the *Addams Family*?

69

In *Point Break*, when Patrick Swayze and his group rob banks, what disguises do they wear?

70

What is Robin Williams's profession in the 1990 film *Cadillac Man*?

71

In *Russia House*, to whom does Sean Connery comment that she looks like Russia's answer to "Venus de Milo"?

72

What actresses play the roles of Gary Oldman's wife and sister in the 1990 film *Chattahoochee*?

73

Who portrays a straight-arrow, FBI agent in *Flashback*?

74

Identify the 1990 film in which Stacy Keach plays a maniacal high-school principal.

75

In *Coup de Ville*, three brothers drive their father's car from Detroit to what destination?

76

What 1970s real-life kidnap victim makes an appearance in John Water's film *Cry-Baby*?

77

Who were the co-authors of *Days of Thunder*?

78

In the 1990 film *Dick Tracy*, what hilarious character does Al Pacino play?

79

Name the movie in which Jack Nicholson asks: "Where does he get all those wonderful toys"?

80

What Bruce Willis film is based on Walter Wager's novel *58 Minutes*?

81

Name the comedy starring Elizabeth Perkins about a woman who accidentally kills her much-hated sister?

82

Who plays Ernie in *Ernest Goes to Jail*?

83

Everybody Wins, with Nick Nolte and Debra Winger, is based on a one-act play by what well-known playwright?

84

Who performed one-handed push-ups at the Academy Awards in the early 90s?

85

Who played Roy Scheider's commanding general in *The Fourth War*?

86

In *The Freshman*, Matthew Broderick is a film student at what university?

87

For what movie and for which character did Anthony Hopkins win the Academy Award as Best Actor?

88

In *Ghost Dad*, how does Bill Cosby die?

89

In the movie *Gremlins 2, The New Batch*, who plays the genetic scientist?

90

After *The Exorcist*, what movie marked director William Freidkin's return to horror films?

91

In The Freshman, what kind of creature is Matthew Broderick assigned to protect?

92

In The Handmaid's Tale, who plays the jealous, infertile wife of Robert Duvall?

93

Name the animated 1990 film that featured voices by Irene Cara, Ed Asner, Carol Channing, Dom DeLuise, Malcolm McDowell, and Phyllis Diller.

94

In Hard to Kill, police detective Steven Seagal is awakened from a coma and seeks revenge. How long was he in the coma?

95

In what country was Headhunter, with Kay Lenz and Wayne Crawford, filmed?

left to right: Brooke Shields, Loni Anderson, Bob Hope, Phyllis Diller and Dorothy Lamour

96

In *Homer and Eddie*, what childhood accident caused James Belushi to become mentally impaired?

97

What imaginative comedy served as a debut for writer/director Reginald Hudlin?

98

Who played the Lawnmower Man?

177

99

What star plays the corrupt cop in *Internal Affairs*?

100

Name the film in which Marlo Thomas, who plays a mystic, becomes the target of a killer who murdered the prostitute next door.

The Toughest
Teasers in
Tinsel Town

1

Name the actress and actor/director who have a child named "Satchel."

2

What film star's father worked as a school superintendent? (He starred in The Roman Spring of Mrs. Stone.)

3

To whom was Mickey Rooney married for only sixteen months? She was the first of his many wives.

4

Name the actor who said: "Girls have an unfair advantage over men: if they can't get what they want by being smart, they can get it by being dumb."

5

What actor married Joan Crawford in 1928?

6

Whose 1963 autobiography is titled I Owe Russia $2,000?

7

How did Carole Lombard die in 1942?

8

In what cemetery are Humphrey Bogart, Clara Bow, and Sammy Davis, Jr., buried?

9

Identify the actor whose real name is Alphonso d'Abruzzo?

10

Whose sister married Romano Mussolini, a son of Italian dictator Benito Mussolini?

11

Name the actor whose father was a furniture designer. (He starred in *The Tiger Makes Out*, in 1967.)

12

Who played the leading lady in the Ronald Reagan film *Brother Rat*, in 1938?

13

Cybill Shepherd said: "She had curves in places other women don't even have places." About whom was she speaking?

14

Who won the first Academy Award for Best Actor in 1928?

15

Whose 1983 autobiography is titled *Confessions of an Actor*?

16

What former child star ran for Congress in 1967?

17

Before trying movies, name the actor who held many jobs, including that of a toy demonstrator.

18

What actor, married to Shirley Jones, died in a 1976 fire?

19

Who said: "The whole world is three drinks behind. If everybody in the world would take three drinks, we would have no trouble"?

20

At what age did Jean Harlow die?

21

What is the real last name for John and Lionel Barrymore?

22

Name the actor who claims his ancestry can be traced back to England's royal House of Lancaster.

23

What actor, successful in both movies and in a long-running TV sitcom, is the son of a Canadian army signal corps officer?

24

What were the five Marx Brothers's real first names?

25

What actress is a first cousin of Israel's former prime minister, Shimon Peres?

26

Name the famous director who attended Pennsylvania Military Academy.

27

How many times has Cher's mother been married?

28

This famous actor has two tattoos that read, "Mum & Dad" and "Scotland Forever." What is his name?

29

Who cleverly remarked: "For a man who has been dead for fifteen years, I am in remarkable health"?

30

At what age did Tatum O'Neal win the Best Supporting Actress Academy Award in 1973 for *Paper Moon*?

31

How did Jayne Mansfield die in 1967?

32

What brilliant director claimed to have a phobia of policemen?

33

What celebrity's license plate has read: "DRUNKY"?

Jayne Mansfield

34

Name the cemetery in which Cecil B. DeMille, Douglas Fairbanks, Sr., D. W. Griffith, and Rudolph Valentino are buried?

35

What actress attended Lycée Français and Yale University?

36

How many times did Clark Gable marry?

37

Who boasted: "I gargle with whiskey several times a day and I haven't had a cold in years"?

38

Name the actor who, before breaking into the film industry, worked as a fruit picker in a kibbutz.

39

What is the title of Edward G. Robinson's autobiography?

40

Name the actress who appeared as a man in *The Year of Living Dangerously*.

41

Who won the first Best Actress Academy Award in 1928?

42

What is the name of Clint Eastwood's inn in Carmel, California?

43

Who announced: "My mother loved children—she would have given anything if I had been one"?

44

How long were Rudolph Valentino and Jean Acker married?

45

Who became the mayor of Palm Springs, California, in 1988?

46

Who played Ugarte in *Casablanca*?

47

Who portrayed the Corleone family lawyer in *The Godfather*?

48

What film had characters with the last names Allnut and Sayer?

49

In *Star Wars*, what mysterious figure is Luke Skywalker's father?

50

What British star was awarded the Academy Award for Best Actor in 1976, posthumously?

51

What country has the most movie theaters?

52

In the Dirty Harry films, what kind of gun does Clint Eastwood carry?

53

What was Herby in the Disney film *The Love Bug*?

54

Who was buried in the black cape he made famous on the screen?

55

In what 1915 film did W. C. Fields make his debut?

56

Who was known as "The Peekaboo Girl"?

57

In what hotel were the Academy Awards first presented on May 16, 1929?

58

Identify the person who said of Judy Garland: "When she was sad, she was sadder than anyone."

59

In what film did Jack Lemmon race a Hannibal Twin B?

60

How many hard boiled eggs did Cool Hand Luke bet he could eat in an hour?

61

Who played the title role in the 1940 film Young Tom Edison?

62

Who directed Kirk Douglas in Spartacus?

190

63

Pickfair was the name of a mansion owned by what Hollywood couple?

64

Who signed Clark Gable's discharge from the U.S. military?

65

In *Casablanca*, what is the name of Humphrey Bogart's club?

66

Who won the Best Actress Oscar in 1963 for her performance in *Hud*?

67

What father and son won Oscars for *The Treasure of the Sierra Madre*?

68

In *The Great Escape*, how many prisoners made it to freedom?

69

What 1963 film cost $28 million?

70

What film was Grace Kelly filming in Monaco when she met Prince Rainier?

71

What actor was asked by Mae West to "come up and see me sometime"?

72

How tall is an Academy award?

73

Who served as director for *Easy Rider*?

74

Who won the 1965 Best Actor Oscar for the film *Cat Ballou*?

Jimmy Stewart and Grace Kelly

75

During WWII, what were Oscars made of?

76

What was the name of Butterfly McQueen's character in *Gone With the Wind*?

77

"Laura's Theme" is the theme song for what movie?

78

What is the name of the MGM lion?

79

In *The Mouse That Roared*, on what country does Grand Fenwick declare war?

80

Who was known as the "It" girl?

81

Name Lauren Bacall's first husband.

82

Who was the Chinese film actress who became Mao Tsetung's fourth wife?

194

83

In what film do stars Steve McQueen and Edward G. Robinson play stud poker?

84

Identify the three acting Redgraves.

85

Who directed and wrote *American Graffiti*?

86

Who is considered the "First Lady of the American stage"?

87

Who did David Carradine portray in the film *Bound for Glory*?

88

In *Cool Hand Luke*, what crime did Paul Newman commit?

89

In *Jezebel*, what was the color of the gown that Bette Davis wore to a society ball that created a scandal?

90

Name the film in which James Cagney portrayed Admiral William F. Halsey.

91

Who emceed the 1955 Academy Awards?

92

In *The Court Martial of Billy Mitchell*, starring Gary Cooper in the title role, why was the U.S. general court-martialed?

93

In what kind of car did James Dean die?

94

On what does the Oscar Award stand?

196

95

What was on the menu when Bette Davis served Joan Crawford lunch in *What Ever Happened to Baby Jane?*

96

Who said: "I never met a man I didn't like"?

97

What actress starred in the movie *The Singing Nun*?

98

What 1921 film catapulted Rudolph Valentino to fame?

99

What actress was the sister of burlesque performer Gypsy Rose Lee?

100

What was the Beatles's first film?

101

Identify the radio and television personality who appears as himself in the 1991 film *Twenty-ninth Street*.

102

What is the name of Warren Beatty's older sister?

103

In what 1936 movie does Allan Jones play opposite Irene Dunne?

104

Who co-stars with Jeanette MacDonald in the 1937 movie *Firefly*?

105

What actor's stage name is John Hamilton?

106

Name the actor who starred in The Yellow Rolls Royce and A Guide for the Married Man.

107

This radio and TV personality made a cameo appearance in the 1943 film Stage Door. Name her.

Answers

The 1920s

1 The Jazz Singer
2 Noah Beery
3 It
4 Johnny Mack Brown
5 John Gilbert
6 Untamed
7 Charles Buddy Rogers and Richard Arlen
8 b) Janet Gaynor
9 Ramon Novarro
10 b) Clara Bow
11 Lon Chaney, Sr.
12 Wings
13 Mary Pickford
14 The Singing Fool
15 Broadway Melody
16 The Cat and the Canary
17 Champagne
18 The Cocoanuts
19 College
20 b) Clara Bow

21 Behind the Front
22 John Barrymore
23 John Gilbert and Renée Adoree
24 Blackmail
25 e) Rudolph Valentino

The 1930s

1   The Great O'Malley
2   Ruby Keeler, Joan Blondell, and Aline MacMahon
3   Edgar Bergen, for creating the ventriloquist dummy Charlie McCarthy
4   Dancing Lady
5   c) It Happened One Night
6   A Day at the Races
7   Laurence Olivier
8   Robert Armstrong and Bruce Cabot
9   Born to Dance
10 Fredric March, Dr. Jekyll and Mr. Hyde
11 The Champ
12 Dinner at Eight
13 Elephant Boy
14 Bette Davis and Fay Bainter
15 One in a Million
16 Constance Bennett
17 In Old Chicago
18 Camille
19 Rose Marie

Stan Laurel and Oliver Hardy

20 Ann Darrow
21 *Sons of the Desert*
22 *Whoopie*
23 Marlene Dietrich
24 David O. Selznick
25 *She Done Him Wrong*
26 Sonja Henie
27 Myrna Loy
28 e) *The Life of Emile Zola*
29 Claudette Colbert
30 *Dishonored*
31 Johnny Weissmuller and Maureen O'Sullivan
32 *She Done Him Wrong*
33 *I Am a Fugitive from a Chain Gang*
34 Jack Benny and Joan Bennett
35 *Curley Top*
36 *It Happened One Night*
37 Noah Beery
38 *The Blue Angel*
39 Spencer Tracy
40 *Captains Courageous* and *Boys' Town*
41 *City Lights*
42 *Footlight Parade*
43 Gary Cooper
44 *A Devil with Women*
45 *Born to Dance*
46 Charles Laughton
47 Frank Morgan
48 Jimmy Durante
49 *The Sin of Madelon Claudet*
50 *Morning Glory*

Gary Cooper and Teresa Wright

51   Harriet Hilliard

52   Fredric March

53   Broadway Melody of 1938

54   Crime School

55   five: Professor Marvel, The Wizard, the Gatesman, the Driver of the Horse of a Different Color, the Wizard's Guard

56   Claude Rains

57   Ricardo Cortez

58   The Thin Man

59   James Cagney

60 Magnificent Obsession
61 Up the River
62 Wuthering Heights
63 Mae West
64 Gunga Din
65 Captain Blood
66 The Hunchback of Notre Dame
67 The Rains Came
68 Beau Geste
69 Test Pilot
70 e) Robert Donat
71 Lost Horizon
72 Ray Bolger
73 c) Pennies from Heaven
74 Flying Down to Rio
75 Tyrone Power
76 b) Public Enemy
77 Bullets or Ballots
78 Anthony Quinn
79 d) Richard Dix
80 Thomas Mitchell
81 Henry Hull
82 Dames

The 1940s

21 Song of the South
22 Bela Lugosi and Lon Chaney
23 Evelyn Keyes
24 *Above Suspicion*
25 Loretta Young
26 e) Humphrey Bogart
27 Christopher Lee
28 *Genius at Work*
29 Shirley Temple
30 *Million Dollar Weekend*
31 b) *The Red Pony*
32 *Fantasia*
33 *Dead Man's Eyes*
34 Polly Ann Young
35 Gene Kelly and Judy Garland
36 Frank Capra
37 Jessica Tandy
38 *Comrade X*
39 Orson Welles
40 *My Friend Irma*
41 John Derek
42 Charles Bickford
43 Ronald Colman
44 *I'll Be Seeing You*
45 *That Night in Rio*
46 *The Outlaw*
47 Errol Flynn
48 *Yankee Doodle Dandy*
49 W. C. Fields to Mae West
50 *A Guy Named Joe*
51 *The Outlaw*

52   Edward Arnold
53   Harold Russell
54   *The Strawberry Blonde*
55   Raymond Massey
56   Joan Leslie and Ida Lupino
57   *The Man Who Came to Dinner*
58   "On the Atcheson, Topeka and Santa Fe"
59   *For Me and My Gal*
60   *One Night in the Tropics*
61   *The Egg and I*, Marjorie Main and Percy Kilbride
62   Ginger Rogers and Ray Milland
63   Laurence Olivier
64   *God Bless America*
65   *Our Town*
66   *The Killers*
67   *On the Town*
68   Dick Powell and Joan Blondell
69   Rise Stevens
70   Vivien Leigh and Laurence Olivier
71   Dean Stockwell
72   *It Happened in Brooklyn*
73   Al Jolson as a boy
74   *The Song of Bernadette*
75   Ingrid Bergman
76   Dennis O'Keefe
77   Walter Brennan
78   Laurence Olivier
79   *All the King's Men*
80   *Casablanca*
81   Rick Blaine
82   Martha Scott

83 Jeanette Noland
84 Judy Canova
85 *Birth of the Blues*
86 Jon Hall
87 Scotty Beckett
88 b) The Algonquin Hotel
89 *To Have and Have Not*
90 *The Great Dictator*
91 c) Lana Turner
92 Criss Cross/Anthony Curtis
93 *The Horn Blows at Midnight*
94 Alice Faye
95 *Look for the Silver Lining*
96 b) Ingrid Bergman
97 *My Sister Eileen*
98 Walter Brennan
99 Nelson Eddy
100 *A Guy Named Joe*

The 1950s

1. Alec Guiness
2. Barbara Graham
3. Cecil B. DeMille
4. The Creature from the Black Lagoon
5. High Noon
6. Joseph Cotten, Marlene Deitrich, Mercedes Mc-Cambridge
7. Sayonara
8. Miyoshi Umeki
9. Marilyn Monroe
10. Kathryn Grayson
11. Susan Hayward, I Want to Live
12. The Creature from the Black Lagoon
13. "Do Not Forsake Me, Oh My Darlin' "
14. How to Marry a Millionaire
15. c) Vivien Leigh
16. Joanne Woodward
17. Howard Keel
18. The Defiant Ones
19. Raymond Burr

20 Abbott and Costello
21 Clifton Webb
22 Rock, Rock, Rock
23 Old Yellow Stain
24 Simone Signoret
25 Susan Strasberg
26 Steve Reeves
27 *We're No Angels*
28 *Meet Danny Wilson*
29 Brandon DeWilde and Jack Palance, *Shane*
30 Born Yesterday
31 Peggy Lee
32 Love Me Tender
33 *Showboat*
34 Gordon Scott
35 Patty McCormack
36 *And God Created Woman*
37 The Moon Is Blue
38 Anthony Quinn
39 Shirley Booth
40 Born Yesterday
41 Halls of Montezuma
42 Billy Wilder
43 The Seven Little Foxes
44 José Ferrer
45 The Actress
46 Corey Allen
47 *Captain Carey, USA*
48 Burt Lancaster
49 Otto Preminger
50 Fred Astaire and Red Skelton

51 The *Actress*

52 Claire Bloom

53 *Suddenly, Last Summer*

54 Peter Ustinov

55 Gregory Peck and Susan Hayward

56 Yul Brynner and Gina Lollobrigida

57 Eli Wallach

58 *20,000 Leagues Under the Sea*

59 Errol Flynn and Dean Stockwell

60 Jim Stark

61 Sandra Dee

62 *The Country Girl*

63 *How to Marry a Millionaire*

64 Janet Leigh

65 *The 30 Foot Bride of Candy Rock*

66 James Byron, *Sailor Beware*

67 *The High and the Mighty*

68 Mario Lanza

69 *Pete Kelly's Blues*

70 *Witness for the Prosecution*

71 Eddie Cantor

72 *Unchained*

73 *Detective Story*

74 *Artists and Models*

75 *The Day the Earth Stood Still*

76 Rosemary Clooney and Vera-Ellen

77 b) Charlton Heston, *Ben Hur*

78 *Sabrina*

79 *Summer Stock*

80 David Niven

81 Michael Landon

82 Kiss Me Kate

83 Jan Stearling and Mona Freeman

84 Jim Backus

85 Kay Thompson

86 Donna Reed

87 Giant

88 Rita Hayworth

89 a) Humphrey Bogart, *African Queen*

90 Too Much, Too Soon

91 Marty

92 *Sex and the Single Girl*

93 Guys and Dolls

94 *A Star is Born*

95 Steve Allen

96 Niagara Falls

97 *The Great Caruso*

98 Fraser Heston

99 *The Girl Can't Help It*

100 Magambo

101 Claudette Colbert

102 How to Be Very, Very Popular

103 Natalie Wood

The 1960s

Gracie Allen and George Burns

21 *Ada*
22 Roddy McDowall
23 Eddie Hodges
24 *Advise and Consent*
25 *The Christmas Tree*
26 *A Fistful of Dollars*
27 *Fitzwilly*
28 Sophia Loren
29 *Flaming Star*
30 Herman's Hermits
31 *Munster, Go Home*

32 Rod Serling
33 *Night of the Generals*
34 *Alfie*
35 Come Blow Your Horn
36 Robert Redford
37 Karl Malden
38 Ed Begley
39 *Breakfast at Tiffany's*
40 Janet Leigh
41 Ed Wynn
42 General Sherman
43 Billy Wilder
44 d) Tom Jones
45 *The Apartment*
46 Monroe and Gable, Misfits; Harlow and Gable, *Saratoga*
47 Natalie Wood
48 Walter Matthau
49 *Spartacus*
50 Norman Vincent Peale
51 Shirley MacLaine
52 Sol Nazerman
53 *Sail a Crooked Ship*
54 Patti Page
55 *War Hunt*
56 Tippi Hedren
57 Robert Duvall
58 *The Phantom Tollbooth*
59 d) Albert Finney
60 *Speedway*
61 Myrna Loy
62 Lotte Lenya

63 Blake Edwards
64 Follow Me, Boys!
65 Follow that Dream
66 James Darren
67 Period of Adjustment
68 Johnny Nobody
69 Michael Crawford
70 Murder, She Said
71 The Music Man
72 James Coburn
73 Pretty Boy Floyd
74 The Russians Are Coming! The Russians Are Coming!
75 b) Jean Seberg
76 Woman Times Seven
77 Jack E. Leonard
78 Chuck Norris
79 The Defector
80 Dementia 13
81 e) Raymond Burr
82 Dial Hot Line
83 Vincent Price
84 Phyllis Diller
85 A Meteor
86 Doctor Doolittle
87 House of Usher
88 Virna Lisi
89 Spencer Tracy
90 Number One
91 Dick Van Dyke
92 13 Ghosts
93 Bates Motel

94 Rachel, Rachel
95 The Incredible Journey
96 The Lovin' Spoonful
97 Richard Burton and Clint Eastwood
98 Who's Afraid of Virginia Woolf?
99 c) Judy Garland
100 Monterey Pop

The 1970s

21 d) Glenda Jackson
22 Ring Lardner, Jr.
23 James Caan
24 Jaws
25 *Alice Doesn't Live Here Anymore*
26 *Alien*
27 *Nashville*
28 Jason Miller
29 Annie Potts
30 Monty Python and the Holy Grail
31 Moonraker
32 The Honkers
33 Merv Griffin
34 a) Shirley MacLaine
35 *Manhattan*
36 Alan Bates
37 *Logan's Run*
38 Murder on the Orient Express
39 *The Shootist*
40 Billy Dee Williams
41 Callahan
42 Jason Robards
43 *Cabaret*
44 Debbie Reynolds
45 Jessica Lange
46 *Godfather II*
47 Anne Bancroft
48 George C. Scott, *Patton*; Marlon Brando, *The Godfather*
49 *Just a Gigolo*
50 Sally Kellerman
51 Hope Lange

52 Margot Kidder
53 Five Easy Pieces
54 Ryan O'Neal and Ali MacGraw
55 Fiddler on the Roof
56 Texas
57 Carnal Knowledge
58 The Who
59 Jack Lemmon
60 Malcolm McDowell
61 The French Connection
62 Marlon Brando
63 The Sheriff
64 Diana Ross
65 Sleuth
66 Bernardo Bertolucci
67 Salem's Lot
68 Paper Moon
69 American Graffiti
70 Al Pacino
71 Barbra Streisand
72 e) Mercedes McCambridge
73 Mean Streets
74 Sleeper
75 Karen Black
76 Roman Polanski
77 The Towering Inferno
78 Tina Turner
79 Diana Ross
80 The Ramones
81 Talia Shire
82 Star Wars

83 The Turning Point
84 *Close Encounters of the Third Kind*
85 John Travolta
86 *Heaven Can Wait*
87 Sally Field
88 *The China Syndrome*
89 Mariel Hemingway
90 *Apocalypse Now*
91 The Tin Drum
92 *All That Jazz*
93 French toast
94 b) Mickey Rooney
95 *La Cage Aux Folles*
96 John Huston
97 Mr. Sycamore
98 Frank Langella
99 Julia
100 Walter Matthau

The 1980s

1 Steve McQueen
2 Jack Wild Man Armstrong
3 Patsy Cline
4 Lobster
5 *Ghostbusters*
6 Shelley Duvall
7 The Sex Pistols
8 John Waters
9 c) Michael Caine
10 Oliver Stone
11 *Harlem Nights*
12 Thirty-five
13 Sissy Spacek
14 Boating accident
15 John Merrick
16 Peter O'Toole
17 *Private Benjamin*
18 Robert De Niro
19 *On Golden Pond*
20 Maureen Stapleton

21 Missing
22 Julie Andrews
23 Lou Gossett, Jr.
24 E.T. The Extra-Terrestrial
25 James Mason
26 German and Polish
27 Ben Kingsley
28 John Lithgow
29 Glenn Close
30 Das Boot
31 The Big Chill
32 The Right Stuff
33 Mariel Hemingway
34 Jack Nicholson
35 Cher
36 Yentl
37 Tom Courtney
38 Glenn Close
39 Jessica
40 Sally Field
41 F. Murray Abraham
42 b) Peggy Ashcroft
43 Witness
44 Rocky Dennis
45 Kiss of the Spider Woman
46 Angelica Huston
47 Oprah Winfrey
48 Hannah and Her Sisters
49 Captain Ripley
50 Blue Velvet
51 Tom Cruise

52 Marlee Matlin
53 e) Francis Ford Coppola
54 Jessica Lange, Diane Keaton, and Sissy Spacek
55 Vietnam War
56 The Devil
57 *The Untouchables*
58 Rabbit
59 Bette Davis
60 *The Last Emperor*
61 Party scene
62 *Wall Street*
63 *Broadcast News*
64 Dennis Quaid
65 Olympia Dukakis
66 Glenn Close
67 Robin Williams
68 *Roxanne*
69 *Dead Poets Society*
70 *The Dead*
71 *Hope and Glory*
72 a) Stanley Kubrick
73 Woody Allen
74 Cerebral palsy
75 Sweden
76 *Maurice*
77 Nicolas Cage and Holly Hunter
78 Peter Weller
79 Dennis Hopper
80 A wolf
81 *The Fabulous Baker Boys*
82 Jacqueline Bisset

83 The Clan of the Cave Bear
84 Jeff Goldblum
85 Mel Gibson
86 Sid and Nancy
87 Down and Out in Beverly Hills
88 Michael Jackson
89 The Mission
90 Philosophy
91 Michelle Pfeiffer
92 Delorean
93 b) Ron Howard
94 Dian Fossey
95 Richard Gere
96 John Lithgow
97 Flashdance
98 Burt Reynolds
99 Alice Cooper
100 The Last Emperor

The 1990s

1 "Ditto"
2 Lou Diamond Phillips
3 Mel Gibson and Goldie Hawn
4 *The Exorcist*
5 Sean Connery
6 Joan Cusack
7 Sanitation men
8 Melanie Griffith
9 Desi Arnaz, Jr.
10 *Flatliners*
11 Jeff Daniels
12 Sharon Stone
13 Woody Allen
14 Ernie Hudson
15 Robin Williams
16 Tony Goldwyn
17 Susan Sarandon and Geena Davis
18 Andrew Dice Clay
19 Mel Gibson and Robert Downey, Jr.
20 Eddie Murphy

21 Old West, circa 1885
22 *Bad Influence*
23 *Bad Jim*
24 Molly Ringwald
25 Goldie Hawn
26 Rutger Hauer
27 Ron Silver
28 Julia Roberts
29 Molly Ringwald
30 *Wild at Heart*
31 William Baldwin
32 Sam Elliott
33 Eric Idle and Robbie Coltrane
34 Meg Ryan
35 Marlon Brando
36 Tom Berenger
37 Robert De Niro
38 e) Ron Howard
39 Christian Slater
40 Kevin Costner and Anthony Quinn
41 *New Jack City*
42 Tom Selleck
43 b) Sean Penn
44 Chevy Chase and Dan Aykroyd
45 *Goodfellas*
46 France
47 Eddie Bracken
48 Dana Carvey
49 Advertising executive
50 Estelle Getty
51 Michael Keaton

52 Julia Roberts
53 *Freejack*
54 Jodie Foster
55 Demi Moore
56 *The Fisher King*
57 "I Love Lucy"
58 *Patriot Games*
59 Alan Alda
60 Leo Getz
61 Tom Cruise and Nicole Kidman
62 Louise Fletcher
63 Her husband
64 Charles Dutton
65 A frozen cave man
66 The planet is infested with lice
67 *Far and Away*
68 Raoul Julia
69 Ex-presidents of the United States
70 Car salesman
71 Michelle Pfieffer
72 Frances McDormand and Pamela Reed
73 Kiefer Sutherland
74 *Class of 1999*
75 Florida
76 Patricia Hearst
77 Tom Cruise and Robert Towne
78 Big Boy Caprice
79 *Batman*
80 Die Hard 2
81 *Enid Is Sleeping*
82 Jim Varney

83 Arthur Miller
84 Jack Palance
85 Harry Dean Stanton
86 New York University
87 *Silence of the Lambs*, Hannibal Lechter
88 In a taxi accident
89 Christopher Lee
90 *The Guardian*
91 Kymoto Dragon
92 Faye Dunaway
93 *Happily Ever After*
94 Seven years
95 South Africa
96 Hit by a baseball
97 *House Party*
98 Jeff Fahey
99 Richard Gere
100 *In the Spirit*

The Toughest Teasers in Tinsel Town

1 Mia Farrow and Woody Allen
2 Warren Beatty
3 Ava Gardner
4 Yul Brynner
5 Douglas Fairbanks, Jr.
6 Bob Hope
7 Plane crash
8 Forest Lawn
9 Alan Alda
10 Sophia Loren
11 Dustin Hoffman
12 Jane Wyman
13 Marilyn Monroe
14 Emil Jannings
15 Laurence Olivier
16 Shirley Temple Black
17 Dustin Hoffman
18 Jack Cassidy

19 Humphrey Bogart
20 Age twenty-six
21 Blythe
22 Burt Lancaster
23 Michael J. Fox
24 Chico—Leonard
Groucho—Julius
Gummo—Milton
Harpo—Adolph
Zeppo—Herbert
25 Lauren Bacall
26 Cecil B. DeMille
27 Eight
28 Sean Connery
29 John Barrymore
30 Age ten
31 Automobile accident
32 Alfred Hitchcock
33 Dean Martin
34 Hollywood Memorial
35 Jodie Foster
36 Five
37 W. C. Fields
38 Bob Hoskins
39 *All My Yesterdays*
40 Linda Hunt
41 Janet Gaynor
42 Hog's Breath Inn
43 Groucho Marx
44 One day
45 Sonny Bono

46 Peter Lorre
47 Robert Duvall
48 The African Queen
49 Darth Vader
50 Peter Finch
51 The Soviet Union
52 .44 magnum
53 A Volkswagen
54 Bela Lugosi
55 Pool Sharks
56 Veronica Lake
57 Hollywood's Roosevelt Hotel
58 Liza Minnelli
59 The Great Race
60 Fifty
61 Mickey Rooney
62 Stanley Kubrick
63 Douglas Fairbanks and Mary Pickford
64 Ronald Reagan
65 Rick's Café Americain
66 Patricia Neal
67 Walter and John Huston
68 Three
69 Cleopatra
70 To Catch a Thief
71 Cary Grant
72 Ten inches
73 Dennis Hopper
74 Lee Marvin
75 Plaster
76 Prissy

77 Dr. Zhivago
78 Leo
79 The United States
80 Clara Bow
81 Humphrey Bogart
82 Chiang Chin
83 The Cincinnati Kid
84 Lynn, Vanessa, Michael
85 George Lucas
86 Helen Hayes
87 Woody Guthrie
88 Removing the heads of parking meters
89 Red
90 The Gallant Hours
91 Jerry Lewis
92 For criticizing American air power
93 A Porshe Spyder
94 A reel of film
95 A dead rat
96 Will Rogers
97 Debbie Reynolds
98 The Four Horsemen of the Apocalypse
99 June Havoc
100 A Hard Day's Night
101 Joe Franklin
102 Shirley MacLaine
103 Show Boat
104 Alan Jones
105 Sterling Hayden
106 Art Carney
107 Arlene Francis